THE ENTREPRENEURIAL
MOM

THE ENTREPRENEURIAL
MOM

MANAGING FOR SUCCESS IN
YOUR HOME AND YOUR BUSINESS

MARY E. DAVIS

CUMBERLAND HOUSE
NASHVILLE, TENNESSEE

THE ENTREPRENEURIAL MOM
PUBLISHED BY CUMBERLAND HOUSE PUBLISHING
431 Harding Industrial Drive
Nashville, Tennessee 37211

Cover design: James Duncan Creative

Library of Congress Cataloging-in-Publication Data
Davis, Mary E., 1965–
   The Entrepreneurial mom : managing for success in your home and your business / Mary E. Davis.
       p. cm.
   Includes index.
   ISBN-13: 978-1-58182-591-6 (pbk. : alk. paper)
   ISBN-10: 1-58182-591-9 (pbk. : alk. paper)
   1. Self-employed women. 2. Women-owned business enterprises. 3. Working mothers. 4. Entrepreneurship. 5. Work and family. I. Title.
   HD6072.5.D38 2007
   658.4'09082—dc22

2007008505

Printed in Canada
1 2 3 4 5 6 7—13 12 11 10 09 08 07

To Jerry, who believed in me, even before I did.
Thanks to you, both my life and my heart are full.

To Kaitlyn and Jared, the two most awesome people I know.
Because of you, I know for certain that God exists.
I love you both "bigger than the sky"!

CONTENTS

Introduction

Have this week's orders been received? Remember to call sales rep about new samples. . . . Confirm tomorrow morning's appointment. Did I mail those invoices? If client's delinquent check doesn't come in by tomorrow, must file a lien on the property. . . . Check the receivables report for other past-due accounts. Have to be at the kids' musical tomorrow afternoon. Oh! Jared needs a new shirt for that musical! Hem Kaitlyn's skirt tonight! Follow up on advertising mailers that were sent out last week. Get new quotes on liability insurance. Need a birthday gift for the party this weekend. Mail sales tax return by tomorrow! Interview new subcontractors this week. Hmmm. Better extend the employment ad. Kaitlyn needs to get to the library after school today. Need to help her with her report tonight. Can do that while hemming her skirt! Still need to send thank-you notes. Uh-oh, looks like it's time for an oil change. Aha! Here's the address I'm looking for. . . .

Whew! You've just spent a few minutes in the mind of a self-employed entrepreneurial mom while she's driving to an appointment. Now, just imagine the mental list that can accumulate in a routine fifteen- or sixteen-hour day. How does she do it?

While every working mom, whether she leaves her home or not, may identify with the constant barrage of responsibilities she faces on a daily basis, the self-employed entrepreneurial mom faces unique challenges. This woman wears so many hats, it's dizzying to put them in order. And because she is self-employed, the buck stops with her. There's no way to fully separate home and office life. Her "businesswoman" identity can't be shut off when her "mom" identity turns on! Her day doesn't stop when she leaves the office. This busy woman constantly thinks, second-guesses, and reevaluates herself and her position in her family and in society, wondering if it's in her—and her children's—best interests to stay at home and raise her family or to pursue her career through her own business.

Looking back and reflecting on the past fifteen years, I realize that I still don't have all the answers, although I've certainly encountered many of the questions that go along with being an entrepreneurial mom in today's world. It all started in the summer of 1992. I was working with my husband in his business, which he had owned for more than four years. I began to evaluate where my life was going and whether I was steering it or was just "along for the ride." Like most women, I was a thinker, an evaluator. My mind was constantly turned on and tuned in, never taking a break. After much soul-searching and one hard-flung briefcase during a heated discussion with my husband, I decided that I was ready for a change.

While my husband and I had a good marriage, it was definitely not easy working and living together 24/7. I was a vocal, opinionated woman who didn't enjoy taking a backseat to someone else for daily business decisions. And no matter how things may have appeared to others, the business was, in fact, my husband's, not mine. I needed to strike out and test the waters on my own. I needed to find out for myself if I could start and run a business.

A big part of what gave me the courage to step off the curb, if you will, was my husband. I had watched him start and grow three successful businesses in the past seven years, and I had always been in awe of his abilities. If he didn't know something, he learned. If it was a bad day, he made the best of it. If he had employee problems, he remedied them. No matter what hand he was dealt, he played it, and the one constant was his attitude. Problems or difficulties didn't mean things came to a screeching halt. In his life, problems were just something to be resolved as he continued moving ahead. I watched from the sidelines as he turned a small start-up business into a successful, efficient machine, with multiple offices throughout the state. And all this was done with a great attitude and the constant respect of his employees, customers, and peers. Little did he know that all this time he was mentoring a future entrepreneur in me!

THE ENTREPRENEURIAL
MOM

"Okay, I Can Do It!"

I still remember that rainy Saturday afternoon when I finally talked myself into it. But what was "it"? I had convinced myself that I could start and run a business of my own, but now I needed to decide what type of business I could grow, promote, and run successfully. I bought dozens of books and magazines, looking for my niche.

What Kind of Business?

According to the NFWBO (National Foundation for Women Business Owners), 14 percent of women business owners in the United States turned a personal interest into a working business. With that in mind, I began considering my own interests. "What can I do? What do I know?" I asked myself again and again. Like many women, I liked fashion, weddings, and babies. I was also a fairly good artist. But looking around I found there were plenty of businesses dealing with these things already. No, it had to be something else.

Still looking for guidance, I visited a large local bookstore in search of "women in business" books, and even more specifically, books about women entrepreneurs who were also mothers. (You see, I was not yet a mother, but my husband and I knew we'd be starting a family soon. And I realized that as a new business owner, I'd have a lot to handle if I had a baby too.) Browsing the bookshelves, I found plenty of books about women who had climbed the corporate ladder, broken through the glass ceiling, and achieved business and personal successes. There were also a few books about women who ran small, often part-time, businesses from their homes. But there was not a single book about self-employed women working outside the home while at the same time raising a family. I decided, right then and there in that bookstore aisle, that if I ever figured out how to do it, I would write that very book one day.

I still had to find my niche, though, and the thought of making a wrong decision was nearly paralyzing. My previous work experience had included employment at a major newspaper and as a licensed Realtor, but I wasn't interested in going to work for another large company and having a "boss" again. Finally, while thumbing through a national magazine that rates franchises, I saw an ad promoting a flooring business franchise that was for sale. The lightbulb went on. *That's it!* I thought. Because I had worked with my husband in a business in which his employees cleaned, dyed, and restored carpet, I already had some knowledge of one end of the flooring business. Although I knew I had much to learn, I also knew that I did not want to pay franchise fees or royalties to a franchisor. Therefore, I would have to start my own flooring business and learn as I went along. What I didn't realize at the time was how much I would have to learn.

I immediately began learning everything I could about the flooring business, from the history of carpet to its manufacturing in today's state-of-the-art carpet mills. The more I learned, the more I realized I still had to learn. "Can I really jump in and make this work?" I asked myself repeatedly. Doubt plagued me constantly. But, ultimately, I made the decision to meet every apprehension head-on, deal with one thing at a time, and just keep moving forward.

Not only was the retail flooring business a new, unexplored, and scary entity, but I also had to learn about forming a corporation, setting up business accounts and merchant accounts, obtaining liability insurance, establishing credit with distributors, advertising, leasing commercial office and warehouse space, finding installation crews, and many more details associated with a new company! Item by item, I plodded my way through this very detailed set-up phase. At twenty-seven years of age and with only two years of college under my belt, I must admit I was a bit intimidated by the whole process.

The First Sale

Finally, with my corporation set up and my office ready, it was time for the exciting but scary phase: selling! While I had always been outspoken with people I knew, the prospect of cold-calling potential customers was more than terrifying to me. I made a list of possible contacts, including Realtors and property managers, who would replace flooring on a fairly regular basis as they turned homes over to new renters.

Boy, did I get an education my first day out. I found that I had over-dressed for my role as the carpet saleslady, wearing a suit and high-heeled pumps. Nevertheless, I *click-click-clicked* into my first prospect's realty office on Cocoa Beach, samples in hand and a smile firmly plastered on my naive face. I barely got out a greeting when I was told, "We already have a flooring person," and the woman to whom I was smiling went back to her paperwork. I turned on my heel and retreated to my car, where I sat trying to compose myself for the next ten minutes. I actually thought about turning my car in the direction of home and retreating to the safety of my house and the comfort of a slice of chocolate pie. But eventually I was able to convince myself to keep plugging away.

Finally, on my third day of sales calls, it happened—I got my first sale! Sixty-five yards of beautiful gray carpet with that "new carpet smell," and I was on my way. I babied that job from order to installation, fixating on every detail.

My first installation crew almost certainly thought I was obsessive. I knew that I needed to understand the installation process from start to finish, so I accompanied them on that first job, watching every move they made, never letting them know that I knew absolutely nothing about what they were doing. Watching and learning the installation process actually proved very helpful to me. Having an understanding of what it takes to complete an installation helped me with diagramming layouts and calculating material waste amounts, and, in the end, it proved to be helpful even in completing sales on many occasions.

For the next couple of months, I kept up a frenetic pace, alternately making sales calls, receiving shipments, and accompanying installers to the job site to ensure quality. In the evenings I did my invoicing and paperwork, most times late into the night.

Then, six months into my new venture, I got the surprise of my life: The stick turned purple. Yes, I was finally pregnant, after years of trying to conceive.

This new development left me feeling both ecstatic and terrified at the same time, much the way I had felt when I first started my business, in fact. More than anything I wanted a baby, but I had invested so much effort into my business that I couldn't stop now. Letting it all go would be impossible for me.

Most newly pregnant women may wrestle with the decision about whether to work outside the home or not following their baby's birth, but my dilemma was even more complex. I knew my baby would always come first, but there had to be a way to make it all work, a way to be both a mother and an entrepreneur.

The pregnancy itself presented many obstacles in my day-to-day life. Just getting up in the mornings was a challenge! There could be no lazy, slow, "ease-into-the-day" mornings for me. People were waiting for me. Flooring installers needed their day's assignments and their carpet rolls. (Picture for a moment, if you will, a pregnant woman driving a forklift.) There were customers to be seen, deliveries to be taken, and orders to be placed. If I had worked for someone else, I could have called in sick on occasion and a coworker would've picked up my slack. But I was the owner of a new, fledgling company, and there was no support to be had except my own.

Somehow, though, between prenatal vitamins and daily ice-cream rewards, I made it through my pregnancy. (The daily ice-cream runs, however, left me with an additional fifty-eight pounds, so I don't really recommend it.)

For some reason, after our baby girl arrived, I thought my life would be more orderly, especially since I wouldn't be constantly exhausted from trying to work nonstop while I was expanding to the size of a refrigerator. Wrong. *So wrong!* And this is the point where I can now look back and offer "words of wisdom" to those women who also want to have it all—a family and a business of their own outside the home.

While many women are able to maintain a home office and handle their mother role at the same time, my business dictated that I continue to keep a remote office with a warehouse, where large trucks could make deliveries. In order to be closer to home, though, I moved my office to a location only five minutes from my house. I had visions of being able to handle the baby and the business simultaneously, using a babysitter only on occasions when I had to visit with customers. That fantasy lasted about a week! I found that it was nearly impossible to check in deliveries of thousand-pound rolls of carpeting, drive a forklift, and answer a phone while cradling a hungry, crying infant. It was clear that my seven-pound little cherub was running the show and would come second to nothing. So at the end of that week, my husband and I discussed the first order of business: childcare.

Childcare

For decades, childcare has been a stumbling block for most working women. There are certain degrees of guilt and envy that haunt most mothers as they leave their child in the care of another. Guilt because they cannot be with their child themselves, and envy because someone else can.

But the need for childcare is a reality for all working parents, including the entrepreneurial mom. And because the latest census data figures from between 1997 and 2002 showed the number of women-owned businesses had grown by 20 percent, childcare will clearly continue to be an important issue for entrepreneurial moms.

Finding the perfect caregiver is a monumental undertaking. (And, ladies, be forewarned: Mary Poppins does not exist. I know this because in my desperation, I actually advertised for "Mary Poppins to provide TLC. . . ."). There are, however, several options to be explored relating to childcare. First, determine if it is more feasible for you to use a day care center, a private caregiver to whom you deliver your child each morning, or a nanny or sitter who will come into your own home. Each scenario offers several pros and cons, which should be carefully explored.

Out-of-Home Care

If a day care center or private caregiver suits your needs, checking them out extensively may be easier than checking an individual's background. Licensing and insurance are required for these types of businesses, and they are subject to random inspections by the city, county, or state in which they are licensed. While you can check out these businesses rather easily, it is also imperative that you check into the backgrounds of the actual caregivers to whom you will entrust your child's safety and well-being. Call your local law enforcement office to ask how to obtain background checks of each person who will have contact with your child. If you are considering a private caregiver, it is important to also obtain a background check of that person's spouse and any other persons occupying the home. Frequently, fingerprinting and background checks are required for day care workers. If you find that for some reason a fingerprint check has not already been performed, ask for it to be done! You can also go online to obtain a criminal history check of the person(s) whose background you are investigating. Check for information at county, state, and national levels. You will need each person's full name, maiden name, if applicable, Social Security number, and date of birth in order to perform a thorough check. While there is a fee for the criminal background check, you will find that there is not a fee to access the sexual predators list on the Internet.

You need not feel uncomfortable requesting this information from your potential caregiver. Your child is more important than a brief moment of awkwardness, and most people are understanding of your need to check out their past if they are to be entrusted with the care of your child.

Additionally, you can contact the city or county where the day care or home is located and ask if there is any record of violations or complaints concerning the business or individual. And, as a final reference check, ask for the names and phone numbers of a few parents who have used the services of the day care center or individual you are considering.

Visit the day care center or caregiver's home day care without calling first. Stop by mid-morning, after the other parents have already dropped their kids off for the day and the caregiver is in charge. Observe the tidiness of the environment and the cleanliness of the children. Do the children seem happily occupied and stimulated or are they propped in front of a television? Is there a sense of order or full-blown chaos? Are there working smoke alarms in the building and accessible exits in case of emergency or is the environment cluttered? Do the children go willingly to the caregiver or are they timid around her? Simply by being observant, you will be able to determine many things about your potential caregiver's routine and her relationship with the children during an unscheduled visit.

Make calls and ask questions about the cleanliness of the center or home, illnesses of the children, and any discipline practices that other parents may have encountered. And, finally, take the time to talk with the neighbors of the private in-home day care or the employees of the businesses adjacent to the day care center. Ask about any concerns or complaints they have heard concerning the business or the caregivers. Question whether they see supervised playtime outside or unattended children left to fend for themselves on the playground. Ask if they hear the caregivers yelling or scolding the children or if they have witnessed anything they felt to be inappropriate. And if you get negative feedback or find anything alarming in your background checks or your personal visits, don't just make the decision to take your child someplace else—let the parents of the other children know your findings. You may have been the only mother who did her homework, and there may be little children in an unsafe environment who can't tell anyone themselves.

In-Home Care

The decision to hire a caregiver to come into your home is a very attractive option, with many pros and cons of its own. An in-home childcare arrangement will allow your child to stay in his own environment and will be less disruptive to his schedule and to yours. In the mornings, you can get ready for your day and simply let your caregiver take over where you leave off with your child's morning routine. Your child, however, will not have the stimulation of a new environment and will not enjoy the socialization that comes from being with other children. On the other hand, your child will not be subjected to many of the illnesses that children transmit to one another, and if your child should be ill one day, you can leave him with the caregiver at home. Most day care centers prefer that you keep a sick child at home and usually require that he be free of fever for at least twenty-four hours before returning to the center.

If you decide to have an individual come into your home to provide childcare, there are several avenues you can follow to locate your caregiver. The first and most preferable, but usually most expensive, route is to find a certified nanny who has trained in the field. Placement companies will prescreen applicants and send them to you for an interview. You can expect to pay the agency a fee for their services, but should your nanny not work out, the agency will find you another nanny without additional charge in most cases. If you do not wish to go through an agency, you should first try to find a caregiver through a personal reference from your friends, neighbors, or perhaps your church. This way, you'll at least have a reference of some sort for this person and she will not be a total stranger. Still, though, background, criminal history, and fingerprint checks are critical in this situation. Do your homework! Your child's health, happiness, and possibly his very life are at stake when you leave him in the care of others. Take the time to check your applicant's references thoroughly. If there are inconsistencies or employment-date gaps, this is a huge red flag! There may be more investigating to do.

If you feel you are ready to make a hiring decision, have your nanny applicant spend a few hours in your home while you are there. Watch how she interacts with your child and watch for your child's responses to her. If your child is an infant, watch to see how the caregiver handles the child. Is she at ease with the child? Does she talk to the child? Does she appear to be comfortable with the intermittent crying spells encountered with a small infant? Or is she uneasy and irritable if she is unable to immediately soothe the baby? As a mother, you have an innate sense of what is right for your child. Don't be afraid to listen to your inner voice.

So, you've hired your in-home nanny or sitter. Now the probationary period begins. If your child is old enough to communicate with you, it will be possible to talk with him at the end of the day to ascertain how the day went. If your child is an infant, you obviously don't have this option. Either way, it is advisable to consider using a "nanny cam" in your home, even if only for a few days. This small, hidden video camera will allow you a glimpse into the life of your child while you're away at the office. Look in the yellow pages under the various "Security" headings to find companies specializing in this field. While you may feel guilty about spying on your sitter, your first obligation is to your child. Check the laws as they apply in your state concerning videotaping in your own home. In some states, audiotaping of conversations without a person's consent is prohibited, but the video will still be very telling in itself! You will be able to see firsthand how your sitter handles situations and responds to your child's needs, whether she genuinely cares for your child, or if the child is left unattended and ignored until the sitter expects you to return home. In most cases, you will be very pleased with your findings, and will gain the peace of mind and affirmation that you need to allow you to focus your efforts and attention on your business.

Discuss with your in-home nanny or sitter your specific expectations. Have a written set of instructions on hand for this person, detailing your child's routine, food preferences, favorite toys, feeding times, nap schedules, etc. Having the luxury of an in-home caregiver allows your child to remain on the schedule you've set and allows you to come home to a happy, well-adjusted child, thus allowing a happier family life in the evenings for all concerned!

School-Age Children

When your children are of school age, things may get a bit easier for you. However, a whole new set of obstacles and expectations may come about at this point. While you no longer have a need for a full-time nanny or full-time childcare, you may have the need for aftercare following regular school hours. Some schools offer an aftercare program for the students of working parents. There is usually a nominal fee for this service. Be sure to take charge and be proactive if you place your child in an aftercare program. Check with the program's administrators to ensure that all persons who have access to your child have had a background check performed. This should also include maintenance staff or janitors working after hours at the school. If aftercare is not available or is not an option for you and your child, it is imperative that you make firm and dependable childcare arrangements prior to the start of the new school year.

Some options may be to enlist the help of a trusted neighbor or a local teenager who can supervise your child for three or four hours after school each day. Or, maybe you know a stay-at-home mom who has children attending the same school. Perhaps she would be willing to pick up your child along with hers at the end of the school day and watch him until your arrival. (You'll pay her for this, of course. Never assume that just because a mother stays home with her kids her time isn't as valuable as yours.) Of course, if your business allows, you may be able to end your workday when the school bell rings and pick up your child yourself. While this may sound like an ideal situation, I caution you: Depending on the nature of your business, you may not have the luxury of always being available immediately at the time the school day ends. So, have a backup plan worked out ahead of time that can quickly be implemented with a phone call when necessary. Other moms are usually all too happy to help out when asked, and, of course, you can return the favor or maybe keep their kids for an occasional weekend.

When All Else Fails

Even when you think you have taken care of every day care possibility for your kids, we all know that sometimes everything goes wrong on the same day and you will find yourself caring for your little ones and working at the same time. As an entrepreneurial mom, you'll need to be prepared to have your children in your office at a moment's notice. No matter how much planning you do, there are always times when—surprise!—your presence is unexpectedly needed in the office, the nanny calls in sick, or the school declares a snow day. While you may not have the luxury of planning ahead at home, you can plan ahead for unforeseen take-your-kids-to-work days. Keep a few of your children's toys, crayons, and a cuddly toy or two tucked away in your office for these times. Also, keep a spare change of clothes for your children, diapers (if you have a little one), quick snacks and juice, disposable wet wipes for quick cleanups, and a nap mat with a small, travel-size pillow and child-size blanket.

When my daughter was an infant and we wanted to settle her, we played a CD of beautiful piano music by George Winston titled *Summer*. This not only relaxed her, but it was her signal that it was time to settle down. For the first year of her life, she went to sleep in the evenings listening to this relaxing music. If you have a similar routine in your home, keep a second copy of the same music at your office. It may come in handy to calm your little ones; plus, it will provide something familiar and reassuring in a different environment.

When you have to run back to the office unexpectedly, and you have to bring the kids along, there is nothing more unpleasant than tired, cranky, or bored little ones—for you and for them. If you plan ahead for these times and keep the necessities on hand, you will get out of the office quicker and your children will be able to entertain themselves or even take a short nap, just as they would at home. Plus, if they have their own things on hand, the kids won't be as likely to tear through your office supply cabinet, wipe out the memory on your computer, or wrap your office in adding-machine tape!

My daughter, Kaitlyn, had accompanied me on one such quick trip to the office. And apparently I had taken my eyes off her a minute too long one day because I walked into a room to see the back side of a closed door adorned with four-year-old Kaitlyn's latest artwork, and no sign of my little angel. Remembering all too well that I had done the same at my grandmother's house as a small girl, I wasn't really upset about it, but I knew I didn't want to let her make a habit of writing on our walls either. I calmly found a bottle of spray cleaner and a hand towel, intent on having her clean off the crayon marks. I called her into the room, ready to make a point, wearing my "mom face." I said to her, "Did you do this?" Seeing nothing wrong with writing on the door, my sweet, precocious little girl enthusiastically answered, "Yes!" I explained that we don't write on our walls and doors, and that she was going to clean off the crayon marks herself. She scrunched up her little face, pointed to a small area on the door, and proudly said, "But isn't that a good A, Mommy?" Leaning in toward the door, I saw she had been practicing making her letters. And, yes, there was a really good A on my door. "You're right," I said, "that's a great A!" Needless to say, we left it right there, and she proudly led her daddy by the hand that night to show off her accomplishment. (That's when I began taking the backup kids' items to the office!)

There's one more benefit to having your kids' stuff around the office. As moms, we all appreciate those shops that keep items on hand to occupy the kids. And, as a business owner, you will find that if a parent can safely occupy their children, that parent is more likely to browse your shop and talk with you about how you can be of service. The longer they stay, the more likely your chances of closing a sale!

Organization of Your Home and Office

The need for organization is always important, but it is critical for the entrepreneurial mom who works outside the home. Because she wears so many hats, all of her arenas must be in order if she is to be effective. Because I have learned through trial and error, I can offer some suggestions that may save other entrepreneurial moms from some of the chaos that I encountered.

First and foremost, use a detailed planner for everything, be it personal or business. If you choose to use a printed planner, look for one that has the week spread across the width of two pages and is also divided into time increments each day. This will allow you to block off stretches of time and, at a glance, know when you can fit your next activity or appointment into the day. Whether it's appointments with clients, delivery schedules for shipments, meetings, the refrigerator repairman's visit, your son's orthodontist appointment, or a trip to the vet's office, put it in your planner! Leave nothing to chance, assuming you can take care of any added task that may pop up. Keep your calendar with you at all times, at home, at the office, at a meeting with a client, and in the car. You will find that you refer to it countless times each day.

And, while some working moms may find it easier to have a home calendar and a work calendar, the entrepreneurial mom knows that using one calendar is easiest, as she is constantly maneuvering to fit in all her family's needs as well as the demands of her business. The entrepreneurial mom's day does not end at 5:00 p.m. She is used to fitting in her daughter's ballet recital between client appointments, and by using a detailed calendar, she can make it all work—and sometimes it may even appear effortless, due to good planning!

Household Organization

Organize your entire household. This may sound like a huge undertaking, but the time saved will be worth it. Start by sorting through everything in your house. Discard all the unnecessary things you find. Get rid of the books you've already read, the clothes you haven't worn in two years, that old makeup in your vanity that never was the right shade, and all those odds and ends you've been saving "just in case." Discarding all the clutter in your life will allow you to breathe easier and will actually be a huge time-saver later.

Next, tackle your kitchen pantry and cabinets. You know, those drawers that only open halfway, and that walk-in pantry you can now only reach into. Throw out all those plastic lids that have long been separated from their mated containers. Arrange your cabinets so that the most-used items are closest to the front and at eye-level, when possible. Go through your pantry. Group items together based on their usage, such as baking supplies with cake mixes, vinegars with oils, and pastas with jar sauces. Check dates and toss out any items that have expired. Put snack-type foods together, canned vegetables on the same shelf, plastic wraps and foils together. The task sounds mundane, but once again, this will be a time-saver when you can survey your pantry and, at a glance, quickly retrieve needed items. An organized pantry also means time saved when making your weekly grocery list because you can see immediately what you have and what you need to replace.

One final step when organizing your kitchen is to keep a notepad and a pen either mounted inside the pantry door or on the first shelf within easy reach and in plain sight. Train your spouse and your child's caregiver to jot down items that they use up, and then, on shopping day, you need only take a quick glance in the pantry and grab your already-made shopping list and head to the grocery store!

Weekends *aren't* for cleaning! Your weekends should be used for rest and rejuvenation, a time for reconnecting with your family. Try to keep the house clean throughout the week, so your weekends are a time to look forward to, rather than a time to clean the house in preparation for the next week's onslaught. The entrepreneurial mom deserves a break too! Enlist the help of your spouse, your child's caregiver, and, if they're old enough, your children. If everyone pitches in during the week, picking up after themselves, doing laundry, and running the vacuum cleaner, weekends will be more restful, leaving the whole family feeling refreshed on Monday and ready for a productive week ahead.

But alas, it is up to you, the entrepreneurial mom, to make this new, organized household work. By your very nature as an entrepreneur, you already have that take-charge mentality, so use the same initiative at home and organize your team! Use your resources!

Start by having a family meeting. Explain that as an entrepreneurial mom working outside the home, you need your family's help. Be specific in your requests as you delegate individual responsibilities. Even your four-year-old can help out, whether it's by collecting the family's dirty laundry or stripping the sheets from his bed. Your caregiver may have time to run the laundry while the baby naps. Your husband can vacuum after work one evening a week. The older kids can unload the dishwasher after school every afternoon. If each family member takes on a few simple tasks, the family can have more fun together-time on the weekends. And a rested, relaxed entrepreneurial mom is more effective on Monday morning!

Office Organization

Okay, now that your home is running smoothly and efficiently, it's time to give your office the same treatment! An orderly office runs like a well-oiled piece of machinery . . . well, usually. Having your office organized will ensure smooth sailing or, at the very least, will help you navigate rough waters from time to time.

Just like at home, take time to sort, throw out, or organize every facet of your office. Handle a piece of paper only one time: File it, toss it, delegate it, or do it yourself. But, do not, under any circumstance, let the papers pile up. Mounds of untended papers make you less productive and create added stress that no one, least of all the entrepreneurial mom, needs in her already busy life.

Every January when you start your new calendar, take the time to write everything down that you know you can already schedule. You know when your home's mortgage is due each month, when your quarterly business taxes are to be filed, when your state's annual report is due, when your daughter's braces are to be rechecked, the dates of family members' birthdays, and the dates your kids are out of school. Fill it all in now. You'll be glad you did when you get a call from a client while driving down the interstate and you need to schedule an appointment with him. A quick glance at your week, and you'll know exactly when you're available!

January is also a good time to sort your Rolodex. Discard those names and numbers of persons no longer pertinent to your business. Toss out cards of sales reps who have long since moved on, suppliers with whom you no longer deal, and contractors with whom you no longer work. Better yet, if feasible, use a computerized contact list. This is the easiest and most efficient way to keep all of your information current, and it enables you to quickly add, revise, or delete entries. A computerized phone list also allows you to keep a current printed phone list in your briefcase for use when you are away from the office.

With today's technology, you can even enter your daily schedule into your computer and have a reminder sent to you, via your cell phone, of important appointments or meetings. Managing your home and business schedules on your computer's calendar is easy and can be accessed via the Internet at home, from the office, or even while traveling. Each evening, print a copy of the next day's schedule and slip it into your planner for easy reference. *Hint:* If you choose to manage your schedule on the computer, it will be necessary for you to print several weeks' worth of calendar pages that you'll need to keep with you so you can refer to them. Then, once you're back at a computer, simply input any new information or appointments that you've jotted down, and it will be neatly stored in your computer until needed.

Next, take a look at your office, your personal workspace. What does it convey about you? Are there stacks of papers haphazardly strewn about, stacks of unopened mail, yesterday's coffee mug, and unanswered phone messages dated three days ago? If so, change this now! Not only is this a clear message to your clients and your employees that you are not in control, but it is nearly impossible for you to function with your office in this chaotic state! Keeping an orderly personal workspace will be a clear message to your employees and to your clients that you are a woman who is in control of her own show and on top of every detail.

The Perfect Assistant Makes All the Difference

When organizing your office, utilize your resources. An efficient assistant can be the difference between success and failure for you and your business. Hire a person who has a can-do attitude, someone with a positive outlook. Negativity is one thing a busy entrepreneurial mom does not need!

If you are considering hiring a person with young or school-age children, address those concerns that you, as a mom yourself, must face from time to time. Sick children, meetings with teachers, and school plays are a real part of every parent's life. But be careful! Because of the discrimination laws that exist today, this is a delicate area that must be entered into with caution. Check the laws as they would apply to you before beginning the interview process.

One suggestion that may open the door to the discussion of children is to mention your own. All parents love to talk about their kids, and once the door is opened, it may afford you the opportunity to get a feel for your applicant's support network just by listening. While your applicant may have a support network in place, such as a mother-in-law, neighbor, or spouse who can help with a sick child, let's be real here! We all know, as moms, *we* want to be the caregiver for a sick son; *we* have to meet with our daughter's teachers as needed; and, of course, *we* want to attend the play in which our son has been cast as an elm tree!

I have found that because I tend to be lenient in allowing employees time for family matters, when I really need them to pitch in, they are there for me in return! It really is a give and take, and your first and foremost goal is getting the support that you need so you can function as a business owner and a mother. And that is exactly what many of your employees are trying to do: work *and* be a parent! So, don't be afraid on occasion to allow an employee the morning off, but explain that you will need extra effort on occasion also. Most moms appreciate the fact that you acknowledge them for what they are: working moms, just like you!

When considering your potential new hire, look for someone with good interpersonal skills. This person will represent your business and is often the first contact for your new clients. If your clients visit your office, make clear to all employees the office dress code, be it professional or casual. (I have found that "business-casual" often leaves too much room for individual interpretation, so make it clear what you mean!) Look for a person with a pleasant demeanor who uses correct grammar. They are representing the company you have built!

After you have completed the interview process and think you've found just the right person to fill your needs, don't stop there. Call the previous employers and the personal references that your applicant provided on his or her application. With today's laws, it is difficult for a previous employer to say anything disparaging about a former employee. But it is still worth your time to attempt to get a reference on an applicant.

A good office assistant can become an extension of you. Make it clear to your assistant what you expect from the start. A person who can handle situations in your absence—and handle them as you would—is a lifesaver. But be cautious. Your assistant *will* make a mistake from time to time. Don't berate or criticize when this happens. It will create a state of paralysis, in which your assistant cannot function. Instead, discuss how *you* would have handled the same situation, at the same time making it clear that you appreciate your assistant's trying to help out. Remember: The only bad decision is *no* decision. Over time, your assistant will get a feel for how you operate and how you handle different situations. While they will not become your clone, they should be able to stand in for you as needed.

An effective office assistant can handle your clients with ease, making each one feel like your company's most important asset. And frankly, aren't they all your most important assets? Without your clients, you would be out of business. No matter what your business, you most likely are dealing with people on some level, and how they are treated by your staff has a dramatic effect on your bottom line. Instruct your staff to treat the employees of your clients with the utmost respect too, for these people may eventually be promoted and be your direct client. Adopt a policy of "the customer is always right," and make sure your employees are clear on your policy. Additionally, make it clear that only you have the authority to drop a client or discontinue service to a client for whatever reason. As such, let your employees know you wish to be kept apprised of any circumstances that could alter your company's relationship with any client. Both your employees and your clients will appreciate your hands-on approach.

Your office assistant should be able to run interference for you as needed. Whether it is a vendor who drops by unexpectedly or a pushy client who demands your attention even though you are meeting with someone else, your assistant should be able to handle the interruption with ease and professionalism.

And incidentally, your vendors or sales reps with whom you do business are just as important as your clients. Both can affect your business in a positive or a negative way. And both should be treated with equal respect. Make clear to your assistant your expectations in these areas as well.

As an entrepreneur used to steering your own ship, you will need some time to yourself at the office to do so effectively. Implement a policy where if your door is closed, you are not to be interrupted by people or phone calls. Instruct your assistant to take messages and then set aside an hour or two in the afternoon to return those calls. If you don't isolate yourself on occasion, you will continue to be barraged by people needing your time, and before you know it, the day will be over and your desk will still be piled high. When you do work with your office door open, move the chairs from in front of your desk. They are an open invitation for people to sit and chat, keeping you from your work. Be selfish with your time and the way you choose to use it. Once it's gone, you won't get it back!

Your Vehicle

Now, here's an area where almost all moms are alike, whether they work in or outside the home! Do you have empty soda cups, smashed Cheerios, gum wrappers, glitter from art projects, and loose crayons all over your backseat and the floorboard of your car? Well then, it's confirmed: You're a mom, all right! But the entrepreneurial mom has to rise up and fight against car clutter—especially if your clients will see your car; even more so if they will ride in it!

I have only a few words of advice here: containers, trash bags, wet wipes, and lint rollers! Keep all four handy, and your car won't look like you have three sets of toddler twins. Put all your child's toys, snacks, and a spare change of clothes in a plastic storage container with a lid. Keep it in your trunk while you're working, and it'll still be handy when you're running errands later with your three-year-old. Small trash bags of any type serve nicely as a receptacle for the junk mail you sort through yet never take into the house, the soda cups you accumulate, and the receipts that end up floating around the floorboards. Next, the wet wipes—how did we ever live without them? They're great for quick cleanups for the kids and for yourself when you're trying to force down a burger while driving to a meeting. And finally, another great invention: the lint roller. Keep one in your car's door pocket for quick cleanups on that navy suit or pair of black slacks. The last thing you want is to show up for a meeting with pet hair or lint from the baby's blanket all over your clothes!

So, only one final word on your vehicle: Keep it clean and presentable! Like your office, it's a reflection of you. If it's clean and orderly, it projects a positive, confident image of its owner, which is just one more piece of the puzzle that your potential client may use when summing up your capabilities.

Juggling the Roles of
Mom and Business Owner

In this chapter I'll talk about some of the unique challenges that face women who are moms and also own businesses—and some of the benefits as well. It's not *always* a struggle, thankfully!

Identifying with Your Customers

If there's one thing that many women have in common, it's motherhood. This common bond can often be used as an icebreaker, whether you're meeting with clients, attending a school function, networking at the local Better Business Bureau meeting, or selling to your customer in her own living room.

Upon arriving at one customer's home, my carpet samples in hand, I was met at the door by an adorable, tiny three-year-old girl who happened to be haphazardly wearing her doll's dress, which, of course, did not come close to covering her or closing in the back. Her mother brought up the rear, red-faced and mortified, trying to explain that her daughter had been playing with her dolls and decided they should switch clothes. I immediately responded with, "No explanation needed! I have a daughter of my own!" My customer gave a grateful nod and was at once at ease, knowing that I understood the situation and saw no reason for embarrassment.

Motherhhood is a simple bond that links so many of us women, and as demonstrated above, it can often provide a familiar, comfortable basis from which to work. It's an interesting journey, and, let's face it, we all love to talk about our kids! So, don't be afraid to let your business acquaintances know you are a working, entrepreneurial mom. In today's society, it is a fact of life and a source of pride for most moms.

Vacations and Holidays

Just because you are the owner of the business, that doesn't mean you're not entitled to vacation time! In fact, chances are, you are the most-deserving employee your business has ever had or ever will have! Entrepreneurial moms are constantly on the go, intricately weaving business and personal details into one busy, fast-paced life. And, while your business may be in the early stages, and a lengthy vacation may not seem possible, it is imperative that you make time for yourself away from the hectic daily agenda. A brief respite is a well-deserved reward for any mom, and especially for the entrepreneurial mom. Running a business and a home can be exhausting, and a break from the everyday is exactly what is needed to recharge your batteries from time to time.

The one thing every working mom craves is *time*. Time with her spouse, time with her children, and time for herself! The entrepreneurial mom also seeks a balance between business-time and family-time. A family vacation or an extended weekend with the family is healthy for everyone, young and old, and the entrepreneurial mom needs to remember to give herself permission for an occasional well-deserved, restful break. So, turn off that cell phone, don't check in with the office, and just take time off once in a while. It will have been a good investment in your business and in your family when you return, invigorated and refreshed, ready to tackle anything that comes your way!

Opinions of Others

Well, you wrestled with the decision about whether to run a business or be a mom, and after many sleepless nights and much gut-wrenching soul-searching, you decided you could do both. Be prepared! There will be

All entrepreneurial moms find that their dual identities as mother and business owner merge at times, and some of those times are inopportune. Years ago, I had spent many hours preparing a presentation to pitch new flooring to the owners of a beachside hotel. Apparently, I'd had my daughter at my office at some point while my files on this client were atop my desk.

When the day came to meet with the hotel owner, I showed up dressed professionally, briefcase in hand. We all sat at a long conference table to go over the photos, samples, and price structure I had compiled.

After our meeting ended, I collected my papers, tapped them on the table and replaced them in a file folder. As we stood up from our seats, the backside of my file folder was facing my potential customers. The woman laughed a bit, and I wondered what the joke was.

When I got back in my car and situated the files, I caught a glance of the backside of the folder. All over it were childlike crayon drawings of rainbows, hearts, and clouds! Apparently, I hadn't provided my daughter enough drawing paper while she was in my office!

many opinions about your personal decision: your in-laws who were stay-at-home moms "in their day"; the eternal "room mother" at school; the self-appointed "carpool mom"; the "Nine to Fiver mom," who picks her kids up on the way home from work every day. Everyone will have an opinion, and frequently you'll hear of it secondhand. While these other moms' opinions may cause you to second-guess your own, if it's working for you, don't try to fix it!

According to the Center for Women's Business Research, nearly 10.4 million firms in the United States are owned by women and employ more than 12.8 million people. For the past two decades, majority women-owned business have grown at nearly twice the rate of all U.S. firms. In a study of gender differences, the SBA found that, not surprisingly, women and men business owners have different management styles. It was found that women take more time in making decisions, seek additional information, and look for assistance from others when needed.

And, like all entrepreneurs, women are looking not only for income, but for greater control and greater balance in their lives. It takes a special kind of person to be an entrepreneur. An entrepreneur marches to a different beat and is driven by different motivations. So, keep moving forward, keep doing what works for you, and don't second-guess your personal decision to be an entrepreneurial mom.

While I can honestly say that I respect all moms, whether they work outside the home or not, I believe that we are each entitled to our own choices. Starting and running my own business was a personal decision that I made for several reasons. I didn't want to sacrifice my family's comfortable lifestyle; I needed to prove to myself that I could do it; and, very important to me, I wanted my son and daughter to know their mother had an identity in addition to that of Mom. I wanted my daughter to know that she has no boundaries, and I wanted my son to see that women can be equals in all respects. I also wanted to teach my children that anything worth having is worth the effort it takes to get it, and that you get out of life what you are willing to put into it. My children have seen my stress and my hard times, and they have seen my triumphs and my rewards. For me, these are life lessons that I hope my children can draw on throughout their lifetimes.

Networking

If the success of your business is contingent upon sales, networking is the life-breath of your company. Every single person you meet is a potential sale or a pathway to a sale. Let everyone know about your business! Talk to your neighbors, your church family, other parents at school, your hairdresser, your auto mechanic, the hostess who seats you at lunch, everyone with whom you have contact. You need not make a nuisance of yourself, but rather, promote your company and its products and services. We are all consumers, in need of some product or service at some time. Do you own a realty company? Are you an artist who paints murals? Do you have a housekeeping service? Do you cater? Are you an investment broker? Whatever the nature of your business, you come in contact with people who are in need of your services, and, many times, just getting the word out will have your phone ringing in no time!

Another good source for networking is your local chamber of commerce. This group is comprised of local businesses, both large and small, whose representatives meet on a monthly basis. While there is usually a fee to join, it will be recouped tenfold if you make the effort to network with other chamber members. Have plenty of business cards on hand at these meetings. This will not be a time for long talks, but rather a "meet and greet" time that can be followed up on after the formal meeting. When attending chamber meetings and functions, wear a name badge with your name and your company's name. Let the other members put a face with the name, and they'll remember you more easily.

Women's groups, whether charitable or business-related, are great sources for networking. Face it—we *are* great talkers! And, we all are consumers too. So, get out and talk up your business to everyone you encounter during the day. *You* are your best source for business!

Motivation

Self-employed people in general are motivated differently. While the almighty dollar is important, so is the control that working for oneself can bring. Control of finances, control of lifestyle, control of destiny, and control of time are all at the top of the list for entrepreneurs. And the entrepreneurial mom is no different in her quest for these rewards.

With so many responsibilities, both personal and professional, it is easy for the entrepreneurial mom to become deeply immersed and bogged down in day-to-day tasks. It is easy to become lost in the details and "not see the forest for the trees." Therefore, continuing to seek new motivation is a must, especially for the entrepreneurial mom.

According to a study by the NFWBO (National Foundation for Women Business Owners), 46 percent of women business owners, compared to 37 percent of men business owners, have a mentor or a role model from whom they derive advice or encouragement. If you are lucky enough to have a mentor, whether male or female, use this person's wealth of experience and advice. Most people are flattered by the prospect of mentoring new entrepreneurs and are willing to assist when called upon.

Entrepreneurs are a special group of people. The successful ones tend to be self-disciplined, positive, forthright, and direct. But even these people have days when they need a "kick in the pants" to get motivated. Entrepreneurial moms, especially, will have these days, as they find themselves exhausted after being up all night with a sick child then guzzling coffee while weaving through traffic for that first sales call of the day. We can run on adrenaline for days, then finally crash and burn. It's times like these when we must draw on the motivation that got us into entrepreneurship in the first place!

Sometimes it is the success itself that brings the rush of satisfaction that entrepreneurs thrive on. Whether it's landing a new account or sealing a deal, entrepreneurs all know this same great, heady feeling. During the insane, hectic times, it is this feeling that we must call upon to get us through, and it is during these times that all entrepreneurs will find out what they are really made of!

Entrepreneurs are used to patting themselves on the back. There is no one else to do it! And entrepreneurial moms need not be any different. It is important that as an entrepreneurial mom, you find what drives you, what motivates you and keeps you going. Decipher this in the early stages of your business and go back to it when the times get tough!

Spousal Support

A successful entrepreneurial mom, if married, will invariably have a supportive mate behind her. While it is certainly important for everyone to have the support of their spouse, it is doubly so for the entrepreneurial mom. Without the unwavering support of her husband, the entrepreneurial mom cannot succeed.

Anyone, especially a mom, who is considering starting a business, needs to have many lengthy conversations with her spouse, as *his* life is about to change also. He, too, will have to make adjustments and sacrifices. It is critical to discuss everything, including finances, time management, childcare, household chores, and the impact your decision will have on your marriage and the dynamics of your family. Any business, especially one in its early stages, requires a major time commitment. At times, this will be a sacrifice for the family of the entrepreneurial mom, but a supportive spouse can ease the burden on a family during these times.

I must admit that it has probably been easier for me to be an entrepreneurial mom because my husband is also an entrepreneur, with businesses of his own. He understands what it takes to grow a business and knows the effort and the time and commitment that are required. But we, too, have had times when the babysitter didn't show up or the kids woke up with a temperature, and we had to sort out who would go to their office and who would head for the pediatrician's office. This is when a supportive spouse is like oxygen! The entrepreneurial mom cannot survive, much less thrive, without one!

Taking Time for Yourself

It sounds so simple, so mindless. . . . Every mom needs time for herself. Every mom *deserves* time for herself! A relaxing manicure, a warm bubble bath, a snuggly throw and a good book, maybe lunch and a movie with a friend. . . . For the entrepreneurial mom, these simple things truly are luxuries that she plans to enjoy "when she has the time." Well, like everything else in her life, this time never comes unless it is scheduled like every other item in the week! And these are appointments that need to be kept. Remember: Entrepreneurs are self-starters, who are self-motivated and who must be self-disciplined. Entrepreneurial moms must also be self*ish* when it comes to their time!

So use that planner! Schedule an hour a week for yourself. Block it out, even if you don't have a specific plan. Browse the bookstore, get a massage, linger over coffee and people-watch at the mall, take an exercise class at the gym, or simply read the newspaper in peace on your patio. There is no need to feel guilty for taking some "me time." Remind yourself you're worth it. This is not an hour wasted, but rather an hour "invested" in *you*, your biggest resource. Your family will reap the benefits of a relaxed, rejuvenated mom. Your business will benefit from a refreshed, clearheaded leader who returns to the office ready to tackle things anew. And your overall health will most certainly benefit from the stress relief you will feel.

Spirituality and the Entrepreneurial Mom

First, let me make it clear that spirituality does not have to mean religion. However, it has always been my belief that there are many rewards in understanding that there is something bigger than oneself. Whether you turn to prayer, meditation, or quiet inner reflection, it is advisable to take a few minutes each day for quiet thoughts, just for yourself. Your mind will be clearer, your heart will be lighter, and your stress level will be significantly reduced.

If you don't have time at home to take a few minutes for yourself, use your time while driving, while alone in your car. Turn off your cell phone, turn down the car stereo, and reflect on the present state of things, first at home, and then with your business. You will find that ten minutes spent with yourself will allow you to put things into perspective. Your mental health and well-being are just as important as your physical health. In fact your mental state very often dictates your physical health, having a great impact on your overall health.

Health and the Entrepreneurial Mom

It is no secret that being a woman can be stressful! Being a mom is extremely exhausting at times. Running a business, especially in the early stages, can be overwhelming to anyone. And being an entrepreneurial mom, trying to nurture both your children and your business, can be the hardest job you've ever tackled! Therefore, your health must be a top priority!

The Centers for Disease Control and Prevention list the leading causes of death in U.S. women as heart disease; malignant neoplasma, or cancers; cerebrovascular disease, or stroke; and lower respiratory disease. While you have no control over your family's health history, you do have control over your own health, to a large extent! While all these causes of death may not be completely preventable, the signs are recognizable and, if a problem is caught early, may prolong the time you have to be there for your children.

The U.S. Department of Human Services lists the risk factors for heart disease as obesity, lack of physical activity, smoking, high cholesterol, hypertension, and old age. While we all are going to grow old, we do have the means to take control of some of those other factors that could lead to heart disease.

In 2006, it is estimated that 273,560 females died of cancer. The top two causes of cancer death for women are lung cancer and breast cancer. So if you're a smoker, give serious consideration to quitting. And while you're at it, turn to your daily planner right now and schedule a mammogram!

Take control of your health, just as you do your home and your business. Without you, there will be no entrepreneur for your business, but so much more importantly, no *mom* for your family. Schedule annual physicals and gynecological exams. You owe it to yourself and to your children to be in their lives as long as possible.

Listen to your body. Are you always tired? Does your back ache? Are you constantly anxious? Do you have trouble sleeping? While all of these, taken separately, may be attributed to stress, they could also be signs of a more serious illness. Speak to your doctor about any changes in your health right away. You wouldn't put off taking your son or daughter to the pediatrician or running your beloved dog to the vet's office. Your health is equally important. Don't ignore it until it's too late!

In 1996, a few months after the birth of my son, I noticed I was frequently anxious, irritable, and had even developed insomnia. I was constantly hot, my heart raced, and I had chest pain off and on throughout the day. Because I was so busy being a mom and running my business, I ignored my health for months, passing off my symptoms as "stress" and figuring they would go away eventually. Finally, unable to live with the discomfort any longer, I made an appointment with my doctor. After some tests, it was determined that I had a thyroid disorder that had deteriorated to Graves' Disease.

After months of trying different medications, the doctor told me there was no alternative but to ablate my thyroid gland, killing it with radiation. By this time, I was miserable and my body was exhausted from all that it had been through. I was eager to schedule the procedure. Following the procedure, the doctor prescribed thyroid hormone-replacement medication that I will take for the rest of my life, adjusting the dosage as dictated by a blood test every few months. My point in sharing this with you is to let you know that I now realize I suffered needlessly for months because I thought I couldn't spare the time to go to the doctor! Had I listened to my body earlier, I could have been spared months of misery.

Setting Boundaries

Because we tend to be polite and want to appear agreeable, women sometimes have a difficult time setting boundaries for others. If you don't set clear boundaries for all the people in your life, your time will no longer be your own. Instead, time will own you.

To keep from being overstressed or feeling pressured, learn to say, "No." There is no need to follow up with an apology or an explanation. Some of the people in your life will be surprised by the new you as you learn to protect your time. Eventually, though, they will come to respect the way in which you handle the nonstop job of being both a mother and a business owner. So, teach them early what the perimeters are, and they will learn to respect your boundaries.

Now, this is not to say that you will need to appear rude when turning down the job of room mother for your daughter's class or team mom for your son's football team. But you are guaranteed to encounter some pushy people who still want your time and think they can convince you to give it to them. Stand firm! You are in control!

Changing Relationships

As we age, we learn to expect changes in relationships. Many times the changes are a result of the fact that we have changed too. This will become even more obvious to you after you've started your business. You are still a mom, but you no longer have time for play dates at the park or Mommy & Me classes where you would be socializing with other mothers, exchanging cute anecdotes about your precocious daughters. You may find that your new schedule does not allow you to meet your neighbor for a walk while the kids are in school, allowing you to catch up on the happenings in the neighborhood. It may be necessary for your sitter to take the baby to swim classes, because you have to be at the office. All of these things will mean that your circle of relationships will change. Friendships don't have to end, of course, but they will change. And, if the friends were special to you, it will mean that you will have to make efforts to protect the friendships, even though you have less time than before you started your business. Good friends will be aware of all that is happening with you, and they will be there for you, but it will still take an effort on your part to cultivate the friendship.

The most important relationships for you to protect, above all others, are the ones you have with your children and your spouse. If you are lucky enough to have a supportive spouse, he will understand the transition you are going through, and he will be there for you, helping to keep the household schedule flowing. But no one except you can keep the relationships strong between you and your children. This must always remain a top priority, above all others. Frankly, the kids won't care about the business you're starting; they just want to know Mom is there for them! So, take every opportunity to stay tuned in to your children's daily lives. If you lose the communication with them, it will be difficult to get it back! Again, this is a matter of keeping perspective and letting your children know that they come first always.

I had an incredible friend, Anna Berrey, whom I met when our sons started preschool together. She also was an entrepreneurial mom, constantly balancing her role as a mother and a business owner. I always marveled at her upbeat, positive outlook. She had a smile for everyone she met and was always inspirational to talk with. My son said he liked being with her "because she really listened" when he talked to her. She was such a kind person, always taking time for others. She was very organized in how she approached her business and personal life, always keeping the needs of her family first. Her organizational skills allowed her a calmness that was infectious to everyone.

By the time our sons reached kindergarten, this beautiful woman was diagnosed with cancer. And, after a long and courageous battle, she left us, when she was ready. In the year before her death, she felt she had much to do. She wanted to make the transition easier for her husband and her young son after they were left to get through life without the "mom organization" they had come to expect. For as long as her health allowed, she cleaned closets, organized photo albums and mementos, prepared calendars and schedules, and even planned her own memorial service, complete with music and a video montage! She also brought together many families with children her son's age, who would serve as an ongoing support system in her absence. She was still organizing right up until the end! This awesome woman had much to teach us all, not only about kindness and caring, but about how to keep the faith in trying times. Her strength taught us all different lessons. She was a terrific mom whose son knew he always came first. I have no doubt that her positive attitude was the biggest factor in her success as an entrepreneurial mom.

Words of Wisdom

As an entrepreneurial mom, you can apply many of the same teaching tools and motivators to both your children's lives and your own business life. Not surprisingly, the parallels will be endless as you raise your children and grow your business.

I have learned over the years that attitude is everything. A good attitude can help you navigate most challenges. A negative attitude will only hold you back, suppressing results and often prolonging a problem. Approaching any situation without a positive outlook will guarantee less than favorable results.

I have been an entrepreneurial mom for more than fifteen years. I am blessed with two incredible children, a son and a daughter. From the time each child was born, my husband and I have tried to stimulate their environment, their minds, and their spirits in all that they do.

When faced with a new, sometimes scary situation, kids need reassurance, but they also need tools to navigate the situation themselves. I think my own entrepreneurial spirit has led me to allow my children to grow into independent people, making decisions, and sometimes even mistakes, for themselves. But I never send them out unarmed to handle things by themselves! I try to teach them to deal with all things with a positive attitude and to try to work through problems on their own. And they know I am always here for them, which I think gives them comfort and courage when they need it. This has worked well for our family. Both of the children seem to be confident individuals ready to take on most anything.

Below, I will share some of the motivators and guidelines I use with my own children and also in my daily business life. I think the parallels will become clear!

I CAN DO IT

This self-motivating mantra came about when my son was about two years old. Because we live near the water and have a pool, it was critical that we teach our children to swim. (Locks and pool alarms are great, but we also wanted the peace of mind that if our little guy fell in, he could get himself out too!) I felt strongly that our children needed the skills to save themselves in case of an accident. My daughter had learned to swim with ease, but my son was more apprehensive. After months of trying everything from group lessons at the local YMCA to private lessons in our pool at home, it was obvious that my son's fear of the water was nearly paralyzing to him. It was gut-wrenching, as a mother, to see my son so terrified. Knowing I had to help him, I came up with a way for him to take control of his fear. We talked about how great it would be when he could swim with his sister and play in the pool "like a big boy." He soon started buying into the plan! I then taught him to tell himself four simple words before he jumped off the pool's edge to swim to me as I stood in the pool. He would say aloud, "I can do it!" At first, he said it through tears with his bottom lip trembling. But by the end of our first session, he was yelling, "I CAN DO IT!" My heart swelled with pride as I watched him overcome his fear with a renewed, forceful, positive attitude!

We have used those four little words countless times as my son has grown. Telling himself that he could do it has served him well as he learned to climb trees, shoot a basketball, play baseball, and break boards in karate class. And now, at only ten years of age, the frightened little toddler who was afraid to jump into the pool is a certified scuba diver, jumping into the ocean every chance he gets!

As an entrepreneur, you will find that you will need to be your own cheerleader, pumping yourself up, convincing yourself of your own abilities, and patting yourself on the back. When faced with maneuvering through a hectic schedule or dealing with difficult people, simply remind yourself, "I can do it!" As you prepare for the biggest sales pitch of your business career or even as you face the dreaded task of terminating an employee, take a deep breath and remind yourself again, "I can do it!" Say it out loud to *really* motivate yourself (close your office door or shout it in the car). As an entrepreneur, you will find that you must become your own biggest motivator. You are at the top of your organization, and those you lead will look to you, not only for direction, but also for reassurance. So, use this mind-over-matter trick and start each day with a positive, "I can do it!"

ALWAYS GIVE PEOPLE MORE THAN THEY EXPECT

You will never fall short of the expectations of others if you always give them more than they expect from you. This is true with your family and with your business.

I have taught my children to always give people more than they expect. Doing just the minimum is not an option in our household.

One time I realized that my kids actually do listen to me was during our neighborhood garage sale. The kids wanted to sell lemonade during the garage sale to make their own money. I soon saw people walking around carrying lemonade and eating cookies. I asked my kids, ages five and seven, why they had decided to sell cookies too. My daughter answered, "Well, if a person buys two cups of lemonade, we also give them free cookies! Remember, Mom, always give people more than they expect!" My heart swelled as I looked at my budding entrepreneurs! (I didn't have the heart to tell them that in actuality their "free" cookies washed away the profits of the lemonade they sold! I figured we could work on cost analysis and net profits another time. . . .)

Whether it's schoolwork, sports, volunteer projects, or friendships, I have taught my daughter and my son to always do a little more or give a little more. They know to write a longer report than just the minimum required length; they will research their science projects even further than what is required; they give their all in sports, conscious of the fact that their team is counting on them. As a result, I have been blessed with two students who have never brought home less than straight A's as semester grades in all subjects. And the children feel good about themselves and their personal reputations, both inside and outside of school.

In your business as an entrepreneur you will also want to give people more than they expect. This is especially critical if your business is based on sales and customer referrals. If you give a little extra effort, you will quickly build a solid reputation as "the woman who can get things done."

When I started my flooring business in 1992, my job description seemed pretty apparent to me. I expected that I would sell the carpet, line up the installers, and deposit the checks. Not so! I soon found that my job description never really ends; it just changes to fit different situations and circumstances. It didn't take long before I realized I would have to adopt a "whatever it takes" attitude in order to get things done!

It has been necessary for me to personally unload china cabinets of hundred-year-old china and crystal for a ninety-year-old woman who used a walker to get around. I've had to personally remove (then replace) more than four hundred collector's edition plates in their original Styrofoam shipping containers, so the carpet installers could get into a lady's guest bedroom to begin work! I've had to go Dumpster-diving for empty boxes to help a woman pack several hundred priceless Hummel figurines before the flooring installers arrived! I've completed a sale in a customer's home, only then to be asked to drive her to pick up her car from the mechanic's shop! I've personally moved appliances and caulked floors in order to get jobs done that had fallen behind schedule. I've dealt with insurance companies for elderly people following hurricanes to ensure they were being treated fairly.

So, as you can tell, my "job description" turned out to be nothing like what I had at first envisioned! And as a result, I get lots of customer referrals from people who know I'll do whatever it takes to give them more than they expect. Our advertisements now state that we have been "exceeding expectations since 1992!"

IF THEY ANGER YOU, THEY CONTROL YOU

I spent years working on this one, let me assure you! As a mother, we know that keeping our tempers in check is always the best way to react to a misbehaving child. It's exactly the same in business. If a pushy customer gets the best of you, leading you to anger, you can no longer be effective in dealing with him. Plus, you give up control to others if you allow them to control your emotions. As the owner of your business and as a mother, you are looked to for guidance and leadership. Anger gets in the way of productivity and impedes your ability to guide and lead effectively. Anger is merely wasted energy that you should divert to more productive areas of your life. So, in stressful situations, be the bigger person. Keep your cool and you will keep the control, whether dealing with your children or with situations in your business.

WORK HARD—PLAY HARD

This is a simple concept and one that will teach your children the value of hard work, plus the payoff for hard work! The same can be said when dealing with your employees in your business.

Ever since our kids were preschool age, we have planned at least one big vacation each year. As the kids have gotten older, they have been included in the planning of these trips. Although we wanted to expand their horizons, we did not want to spoil our children or have them come to expect that annual grand vacations were something to be taken for granted. We have always explained that because Mom and Dad work hard, we also like to play hard! They now know that it's because Mom and Dad work hard that they can ski in Aspen, vacation in Alaska, and travel through Europe. We also explain that we make the choice to work hard, and that they, too, will one day have to make that choice. We emphasize that if they buckle down in their schoolwork, what we consider their "job" for now, they will get into a good college and be afforded more opportunities later. We make every effort to be honest with the kids when we tell them it will not always be easy, but that if they work hard now, they can play hard later as the payoff.

Because all people want to feel valued and appreciated, you can adopt the same "Work Hard—Play Hard" mantra in your business. Money is not the only motivator for people. Employees want to know their employer recognizes the good job they have been doing. On occasion, try "catching an employee doing something right" and offer your praise and recognition. Follow it up with a day off or a free round of golf for your employee. When he returns to work the next day, he will feel valued, appreciated, and refreshed. And who will benefit from his renewed spirit? That's right, you and your business! It is always easier and less costly to keep an already-trained employee as opposed to replacing him! Employee retention is critical for the entrepreneurial mom!

IF YOU WANT TO RUN WITH THE BIG DOGS, GET OFF THE PORCH

Mediocrity will get you nowhere! Yes, it's acceptable to be average, but you will always be in the middle of the biggest group of people. You will not stand out or rise above others by accepting mediocrity in yourself or in others. And, if you are an entrepreneur or considering becoming one, you won't mind standing out or doing what it takes to pull away from the crowd.

When our children were young, we began taking annual short trips to the mountains in Virginia. We'd rent a rustic, hundred-year-old farmhouse in the middle of nowhere, where our cell phones would not work. We'd spend hours hiking, wading in cool streams, having picnic lunches in the sun, and fishing in the beautiful pond beside the old farmhouse. In the evenings, we'd build a bonfire and roast marshmallows, talking for hours with the kids.

The back side of the old shingled farmhouse had a long wooden porch with two old rockers. We'd bundle up against the cool night air and the kids would cuddle in our laps, covered in cozy quilts, looking at the stars in the clear night sky.

One night, after we had eaten our dinner of fresh trout, my husband and I were sitting in the rockers, each holding a freshly bathed, sweet-smelling child in our lap. My son and daughter were about four and six, respectively. My husband and I were listening to my daughter describe the cliques that were already forming at school among the little girls. She was having a difficult time with this, because she has always liked to be friends with everyone, and now the girls were asking her to choose sides. (I must admit that I was shocked to find this pecking order stuff happening so early in her life! I didn't remember dealing with it until junior high school.) My daughter was adamant that she wanted to be friends with girls from both cliques and she didn't want to choose. Realizing that I needed to give her some tools with which to handle this when she returned to school, I tried to come up with something appropriate for a six-year-old. I tried to explain to her that it is always best to be true to herself, and that if she wanted to remain friends with all the girls she certainly could. I tried to explain to her that it is the people who get out of the pack and take chances who would really make it in life, and that being her own person was admirable, especially when under pressure from others.

My husband, using his UNC Tarheels humor that we all love him for, tried to put it more simply to our tiny daughter. He said, "If you want to run with the big dogs, get off the porch!" Both of our kids thought Daddy's advice was hysterically funny, but it also gave them a clear, age-appropriate picture of what I had been trying for fifteen minutes to get across! They understood that it was okay to be on their own and not "stay with the pack."

And now, years later, our children have called on Dad's witty advice countless times to empower them to be their own person and pull away from the pack, if you will.

The same advice applies to you, the entrepreneurial mom. If you want to stand out from the crowd and make a difference, you will have to stand firmly on your own, secure in your own convictions. Don't be afraid to move away from the group, or to stand on your own convictions or decisions, even if they are unpopular. When you succeed, it will become obvious to the rest of the pack that you were strong enough to stand up for what you believed, and everyone will see that you are, indeed, "off the porch" and shining on your own!

IF IT WAS EASY, EVERYONE WOULD DO IT

Remember, when you are in the middle of a trying time, that "if it was easy, everyone would do it!" Entrepreneurship, just like motherhood, is not for every woman. For a woman considering both important undertakings, it is necessary that she possess many of the same strengths and qualities for each job. She needs plenty of patience, determination, selflessness, structure, organization, and, sometimes, even the willingness to ask for help! So, once again, we've drawn parallels between the two personas of motherhood and entrepreneurship.

Both jobs require many of the same strengths. So, when the going gets tough, remind yourself: "If it was easy, everyone would do it." And don't forget to pat yourself on the back when you successfully navigate a difficult situation!

TREAT PEOPLE AS YOU'D LIKE TO BE TREATED

Whether dealing with your children, your employees, or your customers, treat them as you'd like to be treated. Respect their feelings and really listen to them. This is definitely time well spent, as, many times, people just want to be heard. Whether it's your toddler, your teenager, an employee, or a customer, I guarantee that treating them as you'd like to be treated will go a long way toward resolving most any situation.

When you arrive home after a long day only to be met by your sitter who is eager to pass off your whiny toddler, you will, at first try to soothe your baby. After twenty minutes with no letup in sight to the incessant crying, you will no doubt begin to feel stressed at some level. Resist this urge and stay in control. Take a moment to consider how your little girl feels and what she really wants, although she can't explain it herself. Take a breath and downshift into Mom gear. At some point you, too, have felt irritable and overstressed. Chances are, she needs just what you needed—a warm bath and a good snuggle.

The same approach can be used when dealing with an employee who feels overworked and undervalued. Put yourself in his shoes, let him know you understand his feelings because you've felt the same way at times yourself. Take a moment and talk with your employee, looking him in the eye and really listening. Then, if possible, offer a solution that will reverse his bad feelings. (Remember, an entrepreneurial mom must do all she can to retain her employees, as she does not have the time to hire and retrain new ones unless absolutely necessary.)

Dealing with customers, though, can be trickier. We are *all* consumers and customers. So, it's easy to put yourself in a customer's position when he has a complaint that requires your attention. Act swiftly in dealing with customer complaints. This will let the customer know that you consider their situation to be a top priority. They will know they are being heard, which, after all, is what most people want. If, after reviewing your customer's position, you feel he is justified in his complaint, you must act immediately to remedy the situation. Ask yourself what you would want if you were in his place. Then, resolve the issue and don't stop there. Go the extra mile and give him more than he expected to make sure he is satisfied. If a customer has a positive experience with a company, he will tell someone. If that same customer is left with a negative feeling toward a company, he will tell everyone! So, make every effort to leave all your customers with a positive experience. And when in doubt about how to handle a situation, simply treat people as you'd like to be treated.

NEVER DO ANYTHING YOU DON'T WANT OTHERS TALKING ABOUT

This bit of character advice works for everyone, but is especially helpful when talking to preteens about their behavioral decisions. It can also be applied to entrepreneurs because their livelihood depends largely on their reputation and that of their business.

During "the talk" with my preteen daughter, I stressed to her that people are known by their doings. And that if she wanted to always leave a good impression and maintain a good reputation that she could be proud of, she should simply never do anything she wouldn't want others talking about. I explained that she should always conduct herself in a way she could be proud of if asked about her behavior. We talked about how this could pertain to trying cigarette smoking or passing on gossip or cutting class. She seemed to really understand this very simple message.

The same can be said of how an entrepreneur should behave in both business and personal dealings. Always operate above-board. Adopt an "honesty is the best policy" attitude when dealing with employees, customers, or vendors. And, especially, always conduct yourself in a professional manner.

In the early years of my business, I was attending a large business dinner at a beachside hotel. There were many colleagues and vendors in attendance at this gathering. Prior to the dinner, there was a cash bar open during an hour-long meet-and-greet session. A female sales rep for a large company vending its services to some in attendance had a few too many drinks. Shortly after the dinner began, she became obviously drunk and rowdy. When her male associate tried to usher her out of the large dining room, she stood up, taking the tablecloth with her and leaving the other six people at her table dumbstruck! You could have heard a pin drop as this woman left the room, stumbling on her high heels. Although many of those attending the dinner could not recall her name, you can bet they could recall her embarrassing exit from the dining room for a long time to come! I'm sure she could have benefited from learning the rule of never doing anything you don't want others to talk about.

SEE YOURSELF SUCCEED

I am a firm believer in using visualization as a source of empowerment. It's a big, scary world out there, and if you don't believe you will succeed, then no one else will either! Your children need to know you can see them succeeding as well. When they realize you believe in them and in their abilities, they will believe it too!

Early in my business career as an entrepreneur, I volunteered my services to plan and implement a major trade show, in which my business would also participate. I took on this job, even though I was pregnant, because I saw it as a great networking opportunity. I had no experience in setting up a trade show, but I was willing to learn! So, I began the arduous task at hand, aware that my fellow entrepreneurs and business associates had a stake in the success of this trade show just as I did. I must admit, there was a great deal of pressure to perform, and the fact that I was pregnant made for some very long days. But, the one thing I've always had going for me is that I can visualize the end result of a situation. I can see myself succeed!

While this volunteer position took me away from my business more than I would have liked, in the end the trade show was a huge success, gaining new contracts and sales for all the businesses represented, including mine. Was I nervous about such a huge undertaking? Sure! But because I could see myself succeed, I was able to deliver.

EXPECT THE BEST IN OTHERS

As you move through your dual roles of mom and entrepreneur, keep a positive outlook, not just toward yourself but also toward others. Most people are genuinely good. Most people want to "do good." And many times, people will give you what they think you expect of them.

I have always told my children that I don't expect them to *be* the best, but I do expect them to *do* their best. This has applied to school, sports, caring for the family dog, and even helping around the house.

In my business, I treat all employees and subcontractors as though they have the most important role in my business. They know I expect their best efforts in all they do.

Most adults, like children, will give you what they perceive you expect of them. I truly believe that if you set the bar high, both in your business and at home, most people will deliver. And this is because they know you expect the best in them.

TRY NEW THINGS

When selecting your business, choose one, if possible, that will accommodate later expansion. Select a business that allows you to offer other, related products or services in the future. This will leave you with another opportunity to increase revenues; plus, it will help keep things interesting for you in the years to come!

When I created my flooring business from scratch, I did not choose it because I loved carpet! I chose it because flooring leads to many other areas of opportunity to increase revenues. And even though in the early years I had to concentrate only on flooring, I knew that as I learned the business, the day would come when I could branch out. Eventually, when

I felt confident in my entrepreneurial abilities and in the stability of my business, I decided to expand. We now sell all types of flooring, window treatments, hand-painted wall murals and faux-finishing, and a variety of home furnishings. Frequently, what may have been a contract for only flooring turns into a full-blown redecorating job. The ability to diversify and offer other goods and services to my clients has opened many opportunities to me and, frankly, allowed me to do the things I really enjoy!

So, if you have the freedom to select an industry that your business will serve, try not to be too restrictive. Select one that you can build upon several years into your business. Not only will you benefit, but so will your bottom line!

I use the "try new things" motivation at home with my children as well. Because they have grown up with not one but two entrepreneurial parents, our children are willing to try new things without apprehension. In fact, many times, it is the children who ask to try new things!

When snow-skiing was no longer a challenge, my kids decided they would learn to snowboard, which, believe me, can be a painful and grueling sport for most of us grownups! When they mastered tubing behind our boat, the kids announced they wanted to take up surfing. (Thanks to great attitudes and perseverance, they *both* brought home first-place trophies for their age groups in last summer's surfing competition on Cocoa Beach.) And when swimming became boring to them, the kids made a joint decision to get their junior scuba-diving certifications, both passing the same written test and open-water dive tests administered to the adults taking the course.

Thankfully, my kids are always willing to try new things and take with them their can-do positive spirits. It is my hope that they will always have this attitude as they grow into adulthood.

THE ONLY LOSERS ARE THOSE WHO NEVER TRY

Children of entrepreneurs grow up watching their parents chart their own course, controlling their own destiny. While the children may learn by "what they live," becoming an independent spirit is not an accident, nor does it occur through osmosis! It's a journey that even the children may not realize they are on, but one from which they cannot help but learn. You will find that in many instances you can use the same words of encouragement and inspiration for yourself, your employees, and your children.

My daughter was a competitive gymnast for more than two years, working out four times weekly with her team at a local gym. When the coach would introduce a new move into her routine, my daughter would give it her all, trying to master the new maneuver. She is, by her own nature, tougher on herself than any coach could ever be. I'd watch her, flipping, flying, and sometimes falling, again and again, until finally she had it. (To be honest, there were times when I couldn't watch.) After much hard work and countless hours in the gym, my daughter qualified for the state competition by scoring high marks in local competitions.

Our family drove to the other side of the state to cheer on our favorite gymnast. She is petite, and watching the walls of the huge stadium rise up around her, I must admit that I was nervous. At the end of the competition, she had placed, but with lower scores than she'd hoped to earn. As we walked to our car after the awards ceremony, I was thinking of ways to console my daughter, when her little brother said he was sorry she didn't win. She firmly replied, "Hey, the only losers are the ones who didn't try. I gave it my best try!" What a great feeling that was to hear her repeat the very words her dad and I had told her for years. I knew then and there that she would always be a winner. (And that our car trip home was going to be easier than I had anticipated!)

TRUST YOURSELF

Just like when you were a new mom, you will have moments of doubt as a new entrepreneur. Very simply, as you did when you brought that tiny bundle home from the hospital, learn to trust yourself. Usually, in making tough decisions, if it "feels right," then it is right. That goes for being a mom or being an entrepreneur. You will make mistakes along the way in your business, just like you will as a mother, but if you listen to your heart and trust yourself, most things work out in the end.

The Positives and the Negatives

For every positive, there is a negative. For every action, there is an equal and opposite reaction. Many aspects of being an entrepreneurial mom illustrate both of these truisms. As an entrepreneurial mom, you will have control over your own earnings, but this will also mean that *you* must generate the revenues with which you will pay your own salary. Just showing up to the office for forty hours per week will not ensure your paycheck! No longer are you just a cog in the wheel. Instead, you are "the wheel" itself! And while this position will leave you with many benefits and much flexibility, being an entrepreneurial mom also comes with more "pressure to perform" than you've ever known as someone else's employee.

Many entrepreneurial moms decide to venture down the road of self-employment for the same reasons. They're seeking flexibility in their lives, greater financial reward than they could find as someone else's employee, and, often, the pursuit of a personal dream. Many of today's entrepreneurial moms started their businesses *because* they were moms. As such, they encountered a problem and came up with a way to solve it through a simple invention. Because women are thinkers, we process ideas constantly. Because we are moms, we learn to problem solve on a daily basis, sometimes out of sheer necessity! Many moms have found entrepreneurial success by coming up with solutions to everyday dilemmas that they've encountered. Some of the simplest ideas have generated millions for their inventors, simply because someone had the gumption to pursue their idea one step further!

Like all entrepreneurs, entrepreneurial moms seek financial control and, moreover, financial freedom. Reaching the goal of financial independence has many obvious rewards. The drawback, if it can be considered one, is that the entrepreneurial mom must be the impetus and the catalyst for her own success. Successful entrepreneurs, however, *enjoy* rising to this challenge, instigating their own success as they keep their eye on the prize.

An additional pressure felt by many entrepreneurial moms is the realization that they are not only responsible for their own financial success but that of their employees as well. Because we are nurturers, it is understandable that entrepreneurial moms feel a responsibility for their employees' livelihoods and well-being. This can be a great motivator, but it can also also be a source of stress while entrepreneurial moms build their business. As such, it is critical to make certain that your business can handle the burden of additional salaries. When considering adding people to your payroll, keep in mind that there are two types of employees: those who cost you money and those who make you money. If a position is not critical to the success of your business, why fill it? That's payroll money that is coming straight from your own pocket!

If, however, you are considering hiring a sales employee who will generate revenues and keep the "wheels turning" by generating cash flow, then this would be a good hiring decision for your business. Non-revenue producing employees are luxuries you will be able to afford after your business becomes established.

And when considering whether you can afford to hire an employee, be sure to factor in employee costs over and above the employee's wage. You have other costs for this employee, such as worker's compensation insurance, social security deductions to match, uniforms (if your company has uniformed personnel), and training costs (if your new hire will train for a specific area in your business). Carefully consider your total costs for your new hire before offering him the position.

Another advantage enjoyed by entrepreneurial moms is greater control of their own time. Working for themselves allows entrepreneurial moms the flexibility to bring home a paycheck while still being able to maintain their Mom roles. The flipside to this, however, is that as an entrepreneur, most people find that there are not specific start and end times to their workdays. Like all entrepreneurs, entrepreneurial moms must do whatever it takes to fulfill their business responsibilities. So, while she may have the flexibility to chaperone her son's school field trip, an entrepreneurial mom may also find herself back at the office after putting the kids to bed. Again, it's all about choices and priorities, and it can be a very personal and very difficult decision for some women as they struggle to choose a life that is best for their family.

Some women prefer the predictability and assurance of being an employee, while others like creating their own pace and setting their own goals as they pursue their dual roles as entrepreneur and mother.

Many entrepreneurial moms find relief from their constant scheduling woes by learning to rely on help. This may mean help from childcare personnel or eventually from the employees they've hired at the office. Trust the people you put in place to do the jobs for which they were hired. If they come to you with a problem, don't rush to provide an immediate solution. Instead, step back and ask your employee, "How are you going to handle the situation?" At first, you will have to resist the urge to take over, fix the problem, and move on. You have those instincts in part *because* you're a mom, and as a mom it's in your nature to want to "fix" situations, and also because when your business was new, you had to do everything yourself without a second thought. Learn to let go, and try not to waste time micromanaging your employees. It will put undue stress on you and make you exhausted, and it also wastes the employees' talents if you do their job for them. Try to embrace another kind of motherly instinct: letting them figure the situation out on their own and learn something from it!

Entrepreneurial moms list self-esteem and a feeling of personal accomplishment as two of the positives they enjoy as a result of working for themselves. There is a great sense of fulfillment in creating and growing one's own business.

When my daughter was about three or so, I decided to take up aerobics again to try to lose the baby weight I'd put on during my recent pregnancy with my son. I happened to mention the aerobics class to one of my regular customers one day and she said she'd like to come along sometime. She said that she'd like to ride to the gym with me and take the class together because she was new to aerobics and a bit self-conscious. Sometimes being a mom makes it easier to connect with female clients and customers because women naturally tend to be more open to that connection (especially if they have kids, because who doesn't want to swap kid stories with other moms?), and of course while it's nice to make a friend, the business connection doesn't hurt either! So I was quite enthusiastic about this plan. We decided to meet at my house, then take one car to the gym that evening. Although she had been my customer for more than three years, we weren't exactly friends yet, and in fact, she'd never met my children. As many new moms are, I was excited to show off my new baby boy and my toddler daughter. When my customer arrived at my home, she was wearing a long T-shirt over leggings. My daughter said to her, "Is that your nightie?" Smiling, my customer answered, "No, but maybe it looks like something your mommy sleeps in." Kaitlyn piped right up and in her little, elfin voice replied, "Oh, no! My mommy and daddy sleep naked!"

If, however, you are a woman who enjoys a pat on the back or a "Well done!" from a boss, then entrepreneurship is not for you. There are no performance evaluations, no pep talks, no camaraderie, and no promotions when you work for yourself.

The only gauge you'll have of your own success is in how well your business is doing. Therefore, goal setting is a must. Psychologically, the entrepreneurial mom still needs to see her own accomplishments, just like everyone else. Creating goals toward which you can strive will keep you energized and stimulated. And when you reach your goals and can afford to increase your own salary, take a bonus for yourself, or splurge on a family vacation, it's a great feeling of accomplishment!

Entrepreneurial moms set their own limits, both personally and in business. As an entrepreneurial mom, you will decide how far to take your business, whether to grow it into a large company or keep it small and remain hands-on in all aspects of the business. No matter the size of your business, as an entrepreneurial mom you will soon realize you must constantly reinvent yourself and your business. The marketing plan that worked last summer will become outdated; the products you provide will be improved upon by your competitors; the promotional items you give to your customers will become boring; even your computer system will become obsolete as technology advances. But, these things are to be expected. To be successful, you cannot stand still! Keep moving, keep improving, and stay ahead of your competitors!

Staying ahead of your competition frequently involves continuing education. Even if your chosen field does not require licensing or certification, you will find that continuing education courses will keep your mind sharp and will also keep the creative juices flowing. Look into attending a women's business conference, a seminar featuring a motivational speaker or even a course at your local community college. As an entrepreneurial mom, you'll find that you need to find your own stimuli in order to keep a fresh perspective. And, as an added bonus, your children will see that you value education and that even adults can always learn something new!

Being an entrepreneurial mom puts you in a great position to teach your children about goal setting and rewards for hard work. Your children will see firsthand that you work hard, but you will need to point out why you choose to do it! Because they're children, it's easy for them to take things for granted and think nothing of it when you plunk down eighty dollars for a pair of athletic shoes or hand them twenty bucks to go to a movie with friends. It's up to you, as their mother, to take the time to explain the "cause and effect" process through which this occurs.

As an entrepreneurial mom, you will most likely choose to schedule a summer vacation with your children. Include them in the planning of your trip, even months before your departure. Allow them to help geographically plot your trip, compare airfares, book your hotels and rental cars, and plan the activities in which you'll participate while on vacation. This is an excellent way for you to teach your children how to budget and the value of a dollar. Also use this time to discuss with your children that the family is able to enjoy the reward of the upcoming trip because you (and their dad) worked hard and planned for it. This process can be a great teaching tool, even for elementary-aged children.

I am, in fact, working on this book while vacationing in Central America with my husband and children. Our family had a great time planning our trip, from our air travel and accommodations to whitewater rafting on the Chiriqui River, scuba diving in Bocas Del Toro, and horseback riding in the mountains of Boquete. The kids got to learn about ziplining over the Panamanian jungle before they tried it out for themselves. They helped map our travels from home and then got to try out their Spanish when they arrived in Panama. For our family, travel has provided not only fun and adventure, but a way of teaching our children the value of hard work and its rewards.

But of course, for every positive one can always find a negative. As such, we are careful to ensure that our children do not take their lives for granted. Because we want them to learn money management skills, we let them save their own money for special purchases. A few years ago, the children pooled their money to purchase their own surfboard. And frankly, I think they take better care of their things when they buy them with their own money! Of course, I have to resist the urge to give them whatever they want, allowing them instant gratification and making me the hero that all moms want to be to their kids! But I know the message is clear in the lessons we're teaching our children, as they learn not only the value of money but how to handle it, which truly is a life lesson they will always use.

As an entrepreneurial mom, you will enjoy the freedom of selecting the people who will represent you and your business. While this sounds great, there is a drawback. You will find that in some cases, the best person for the job is not necessarily a person you even like. Not so great anymore, is it? Not to worry! Just remember that you want to fill the position with the person most qualified to benefit your business. Let them do their job and get the results. You don't have to be friends with every person you employ. But you do have to ensure the success of your business!

Owning your own business can be exhilarating. It can also be exhausting. Watch for signs of burn-out in yourself. As a mom, you've been used to handling ten things at once—and everyone is used to letting you do it! As an entrepreneurial mom, you need to be conscious of the fact that if you run yourself ragged, both your business and your home life will suffer.

One positive I've found with running my own business is that each day offers variety and the chance to learn and grow. I must admit that I am sometimes too tired to appreciate all that variety, but it does keep my life from getting boring!

As an entrepreneurial mom, it will be up to you to motivate your employees, just like you motivate your family, and mold them into a cohesive team. If everyone is working toward the same, common goal, you're sure to get there quicker!

Be prepared to deal with the unexpected. Deliveries will be delayed; equipment breaks down; employees call in sick; customers don't always pay on time. As the saying goes, "Expect the unexpected!" Just remember that these glitches are not the end of the world. They're just bumps in the road that you'll learn to navigate.

The truth about being an entrepreneurial mom is that you'll love being your own boss—except for the times you'll hate it! But there will come a time when you realize you're in it for the long haul and you can't turn back, no matter what life serves you up! I know many entrepreneurs and they'll all tell you it's not always a bed of roses. It's stressful knowing you have a constant pressure to perform, and that your own livelihood depends on the success of your business. It's overwhelming knowing that the buck stops with you. And it's tiring, especially as you mother your children while at the same time growing your business. The good thing, however, is that *you* have the power to control your own destiny. *You* make all the decisions in how you'll handle your own future.

When you're first in business, many people will say things to you like, "Wow! It must be great working for yourself!" The reality—for new, small businesses anyway—is that the business owner is also the bookkeeper, the salesperson, the marketing director, the clerical staff, and the janitor. I always loved it when people would say things like, "Gee! It must be great to take off from work whenever you want to!" Anyone who has ever been self employed knows that this is the farthest thing from the truth. In reality, when you're in the early stages of your business, you will work harder than ever before and put in more hours than you had even imagined! But hang in there; as your business grows and stabilizes, you will come to love it once again. As you work through the growing pains of your new business, things will become easier and you'll be glad you took the plunge into entrepreneurship!

All entrepreneurs know that great, heady feeling of making a big sale or finalizing a major contract. There's nothing like it. You set a goal, worked for it, and made things happen! However, for every sale you close, there are several more that you won't. Therefore, you'd better be able to handle rejection! It doesn't feel good to anyone. But after you learn to not take it personally, you will realize that it's just a part of doing business and not a personal rejection of you. Women tend to internalize failures and take them upon themselves. Fight that instinct. Even the best ballplayers don't hit a home run every time!

So, go into business with a thick skin and be prepared to take the good with the bad. It's only natural to feel some disappointment when you don't finalize a sale, but as an entrepreneurial mom, you don't have time to wallow in your disappointment. Pick up the kids at school, don't look back, and remember that it's "just business."

Entrepreneurial Moms Speak

During the course of my interviews with numerous entrepreneurial moms across the United States, one thing became very clear: Successful entrepreneurial moms are willing to do everything and anything it takes! While the women I spoke with had varying backgrounds and education levels, it was amazing how similar they were to one another. All of the women put family first, emphasizing their commitment to their children above all else. They all share a strong work ethic and a desire to surpass the expectations of others. Many of the women have a strong faith in God and have looked to Him for answers and leaned on Him for support during the difficult times. All of the women I spoke with, although most had never met, had a common bond and a similar core of strength.

Linda Bradshaw, of Greensboro, North Carolina, was thrust into the decision to become an entrepreneurial mom, whether she was ready or not! Six months pregnant and already the mother of one young child, Linda was flabbergasted when her husband of thirteen years announced they would be getting a divorce. Realizing she had no time to spare and no time to dwell on the situation, she launched her plan of action. Linda and a friend opened a real estate office in September 2001. Unfortunately, within days of her official opening, the country was faced with that horrific day in U.S. history that no American will ever forget: 9/11. While Linda dealt with the same gut-wrenching sadness and uncertainty that most Americans experienced, she had her own tense drama unfolding at home. She was a mother on her own with children to support, not only financially, but also emotionally, psychologically, and in every other way conceivable. She knew she had to act fast to find another source of income, as real estate was definitely not going to pay her bills in the near future.

Realizing that a job in a department store or a restaurant wouldn't pay enough, Linda decided to pick up some housecleaning jobs, at least for a while, so that she could pay her bills. Those housecleaning jobs led to customers asking her to organize their homes, plan their dinner parties, handle their holiday decorating, and even redecorate their homes. Asked how she got into her business, Linda says, "I was thrown into it!"

And today, as the sole owner of Pull It Together, Linda Bradshaw wouldn't have it any other way! She admits, however, that running her own business has gotten easier as her kids have gotten older. But in the early days, like many entrepreneurial moms, Linda did whatever was necessary. "If it means baking cupcakes at midnight, that's what you do!" she answered when I asked how she juggled her mom duties and her business-owner responsibilities.

Linda explained that she chose a business with no overhead and no accounts receivable. She basically sells her services and collects payment upon completion of each job. Linda said her goal is to always give the client more than they ever anticipated. As a result, she has many repeat customers and now even offers home staging, whereby she assists people whose houses are for sale in making their homes more appealing and marketable, resulting in quicker sales.

Because the bulk of her business is from word-of-mouth referrals, Linda has no need to advertise, but she does market herself and her services. She offers to set up the refreshments at Realtors' caravan tours for area real estate agents, during which she also has a drawing for a gift certificate for two free hours of home staging services. The Realtors are educated about her services, plus one of them is able to present a seller with a gift certificate for Linda's services.

Linda also provides free gift certificates for various group functions, such as the Junior League luncheons in her town. "It's great *free* publicity!" Linda says, "and I always end up with several jobs" as a result of the giveaways.

Linda remarked that she enjoys having the creativity and freedom being an entrepreneur allows. "I wouldn't want to work for someone where I couldn't do things the way I want to do them," Linda said, crediting her success to hard work, determination, the ability to "think outside the box," and the ability to give a customer more than they expect.

Feeling unfulfilled in her job, **Diane Taylor,** a registered nurse for more than a decade, was looking for a change. One day, while at home in Lubbock, Texas, Diane came across a short article in the *Reader's Digest* magazine that offered just the inspiration she needed. Diane read about a nurse who had started an adult day care center for senior citizens and special-needs adults. And so, the Lubbock Adult Day Center was born!

Diane, the married mother of two sons, admits that being an entrepreneur is not always easy. In the early days of her business, Diane remembers praying, "God, please give me patience!" Her best friend asked whether she had asked for patience or patients, and Diane replied, "God will give me whichever he thinks I need!"

When Diane opened her business, her boys were eight and fourteen years old. Fortunately for her, the school bus picked up the boys at the end of their driveway each morning. And because her business closed at 5:00 p.m., she arrived home shortly after her sons did, allowing her to start the family's evening routine. Diane's regular work schedule also allowed her to stay active with her sons as they pursued their own interests, including baseball.

Diane chooses to remain active in all areas of her business, from the financial aspects to the day-to-day activities. "I won't ask anyone to do anything I won't do myself," she says. "I'll wash dishes, unload groceries, anything." Diane went on to explain, "We women don't limit our responsibilities as men do."

Although today her business is successful, it was necessary in the early years for Diane to return to nursing, as her business stabilized.

"Most businesses fail," Diane said, "not because they don't make money, but because they can't survive *until* they make money."

Today, there are many grateful senior citizens and special-needs adults in Lubbock, Texas, who are delighted that Diane had the staying power to make her business a success!

Jennifer Yamamoto started her business, PediaSpeech Services, Inc., before her children were born. She and her husband, also an entrepreneur, are raising their three-year-old and nine-month-old children while running separate businesses in Georgia.

In Jennifer's case, her business was already established before she became pregnant with her first child. She credits an efficient practice manager with assisting her in managing her business. "Don't be afraid to hire non-revenue-producing employees if they can make your life easier!" Jennifer offered.

Jennifer found a creative way to handle her initial childcare dilemma. She, along with two female employees, hired a childcare provider to come into her business and care for all of their children. Jennifer set up a comfortable nursery in a separate office, and the three nursing moms paid the sitter to care for the babies while they worked.

As her baby grew, and Jennifer had her second child, her childcare needs changed also. She used a nanny part-time in the office nursery and part-time at her home. Eventually, Jennifer and her husband decided to employ a nanny full-time in their home. Jennifer said that entrepreneurial moms must be flexible because as their children grow, their needs will also change. "If you can afford a nanny, I highly recommend it," Jennifer said. She went on to say, "Owning your own business means you will have more stress, and having a nanny decreases stress." For Jennifer, finding a reliable nanny was easy via word-of-mouth referrals, resulting from the pediatric setting of her business. "Check the nanny out thoroughly," Jennifer cautioned. She recommends checking the nanny's criminal history, driving record, and referrals.

Jennifer implemented a "Mothers' Morning Out" program in her business, in which her children also participate several days a week. The program, run by a speech therapist, has been a huge success, and now has a waiting list of applicants.

Asked how she handles coping with a sick child and a full day of clients, Jennifer said, "My kids come first!" And because Jennifer's business exists in a pediatric climate, her clients are understanding if she needs to reschedule in order to stay home with sick children or take them to the doctor. "I'm always the one to take my kids to the doctor," Jennifer said.

When discussing the obstacles she encountered early in her business, Jennifer mentioned cash flow and the fact that working for herself meant she had to find suitable health-care insurance for herself and her family. "Don't be afraid to make the jump (into entrepreneurship) because of health insurance or benefits," Jennifer said.

Jennifer said running her own business has enhanced her life and continues to benefit her family. She said working for herself allows for greater flexibility in her schedule, plus the flexibility allows her family to vacation five to six weeks per year. "It's a hill to climb up," Jennifer said, "but once you get there, it's worth it!"

After making baby food for their own babies, **Cheryl Tallman** and her sister, **Joan Ahlers,** decided to create a kit so other moms could provide homemade, nutritious foods for their babies too. Cheryl explained that after she created a business plan and did market research, she found there was a lack of similar items on the market.

Today, Cheryl and Joan's company, Fresh Baby, offers complete kits for making homemade baby food, a baby food cookbook, baby food trays, a how-to DVD for making baby food, breast milk storage trays, and disposable place mats. Their products are offered through natural food stores, bookstores, baby boutiques, hospitals, and wellness clinics, and can also be ordered through their Web site.

Not only do both women have children, but they live in different states, and yet still manage their business. Joan lives in New Mexico and is the director of sales, and Cheryl "handles everything else" from Michigan.

Cheryl, the married mother of a five-year-old son, gets together with her husband each night to go over the next day's schedule as it pertains to their son's activities. Because her husband also owns a business, she says they have some flexibility in their schedules. Depending on their own business obligations and their son's activities, they work out the next day's plans. Cheryl said her son goes to kindergarten two and a half days each week, and on other days he has planned activities or they have a day care available. Cheryl has found that the day care allows her son more socialization time, something she feels is important, as he is an only child.

Cheryl tries to keep to a schedule, making sure the family starts the day with breakfast together and ends it with dinner together. She said she uses dinnertime to talk with her son about his day and his plans for the following day.

"The rewards are huge!" Cheryl answered when asked how being an entrepreneur has affected her life. "I can make my own hours, run my own business, and make my own decisions," she said.

Cheryl credits a "very optimistic" outlook and "above-average business skills" as the reasons for her success. When she first started her business, Cheryl said she encountered manufacturers who didn't want to deal with her because her business was small. But Cheryl persevered. "I don't give up too easily!" she said.

Andrea Molitor, the married mother of two children, owns six Fantastic Sam's salons in central Florida. Andrea chose to purchase franchises, figuring it would be easy to replicate each location and because she liked the national recognition and reputation Fantastic Sam's already had.

"In the early stages of business development, it was much more time-consuming than I ever imagined!" Andrea said. She went on to explain that her salons were open seven days a week and eleven hours per day. "Unfortunately, I felt that with my business being a cash-basis business, I needed to be there all the time until I developed my staff and learned to trust the systems I had in place," Andrea said. She quickly learned that she needed to develop her managers and give them the ability to make day-to-day decisions. "I am comfortable with the infrastructure that I currently have in place and look forward to opening two more salons to meet my goal of eight salons in five years," Andrea explained.

For Andrea, being both a mom and a business owner is important. "The balancing act of mom and professional is an important task for me," Andrea said. "I make it a priority to end my day by 3:00 p.m. to pick up my two children from school," she elaborated. "This was one of the reasons I wanted to be in business for myself."

In the early stages of her business, Andrea tried to also keep up the house by herself, but found that she was giving up time with her family in the evenings. Because it was stressful for her to try to keep up with everything, she felt something had to give. "I do have a housekeeper who comes in once a week," she said. "She is a godsend to me!"

Asked about her role as a business owner, Andrea said, "The benefits in working for yourself are endless." She enjoys the flexibility in being able to divide her time between home and work.

Andrea also feels responsible for her fifty-eight employees' livelihoods. "Success is not an option, it is a requirement," she said. With the support of her franchisor, Andrea "hasn't had to reinvent the wheel." She explained, "Along with owning your own business, you have a network out there of other business owners within the same franchise."

Asked what advice she could give to new entrepreneurial moms, Andrea said, "The only advice I would give would be to create a list of priorities in your life, whether it be for family, child-rearing, or business. Then, work backward and find a passion that fits into your priority list." Andrea said the options for today's entrepreneurial moms are endless. "But," she advised, "it has to fit your lifestyle to enable you to be successful."

Megan Bergerson was twenty-six years old when she started her business, ReMax Metro Properties. She had originally been a teacher, and although she loved her job, it didn't pay the bills.

Living in Lynnwood, Washington, and several years into her business, she and her husband welcomed their first child, a son, into the world. Attempting to ensure that one of them was rested, they alternated weekly schedules of which parent would put their son to bed and which would handle the morning routine. Megan said she is fortunate to have a good support system for childcare. Her retired in-laws care for their son three days a week, and she and her husband handle the other days.

Because her husband is also her business partner, they have some flexibility in their schedules.

Asked what she could share with new entrepreneurial moms trying to juggle their dual roles, Megan said, "Know that it's frustrating and time-consuming. Plan on not getting a lot of sleep!"

Megan said time management can be a frustration at times for her because she must always be "on-call" to her clients. She uses babysitters, if necessary, on the weekends. "It's hard to portray your professionalism with a child screaming in the background." Megan laughed. "And the first few years, you work all the time, and you just can't have a child there." Megan now works about forty hours per week, although before becoming a mother, she worked as many as sixty hours weekly.

Megan said that because the first years in business can be a financial strain, she recommends having your finances in line and getting a good accountant. The owner of a franchise herself, Megan also said she highly recommends purchasing a franchise for name recognition. "It's great to have that big name behind you!" she said.

Although her sons are nearly grown today, **Janine Schwartz** started her business, Movin' & Groovin' Exercise for Kids, when they were just seven and nine years old. Concerned that her seven-year-old son was overweight, she took him to a nutritionist and an endocrinologist. When it was determined that the sports he was playing weren't giving him enough exercise, Janine tried to get her son a gym membership. But the local gyms would not accept children under sixteen years of age. Increasingly concerned, Janine decided to buy her son some exercise videos, only to find there were none on the market for children. Janine knew immediately that she would change that!

Today, her Tampa, Florida, business offers exercise videos for children of various age levels. The videos have motivational messages, original music, lively sets, and easy-to-follow instructions. Already young actors, Janine's sons have always been part of the business. "My life has really always revolved around my kids," Janine explained.

While running her business and being a mother to her two boys, Janine has always found time to volunteer at their schools, even tutoring students. She explained that she has been able to manage her business around her sons' school schedules. In 1999, she was recognized as the Best Volunteer in the Hillsborough County School District, after volunteering more than three hundred hours of her time. Asked how she juggled her many activities, Janine laughingly answered, "By not having a social life!"

Janine also credits her husband with always pitching in to help with their family's needs. "You need the support of your family," she said, "or it's an uphill battle." She said she also found it helpful to have the boys in the same sports, as they grew up, rather than trying to follow two team schedules.

Working for herself allowed Janine flexibility while mothering her two boys. "Traveling was always important to our family; we took lots of three-day weekends," she said.

Janine said that being headstrong, stubborn, and persistent has been an asset to her. "I believe in what I do," she said. "I didn't set out to do this for the money."

"Working on my own has been fantastic as I am able to create my own schedule, which allows flexibility," explained **Kirsten Chute,** owner of Cruises for Families. "I also love the fact that my children see the benefits of my work and know that it is a company I created," Kirsten went on. "It gives them the confidence that they also can achieve their dreams someday as well!"

Kirsten started her business in Hinsdale, Illinois, in 1998 and is the married mother of three children. Her older children, ages ten and eight, are in school during the workday, and Kirsten's three-year-old attends preschool every day. Kirsten works while her children are in school and has the afternoons with the children. "This has proven to be a very effective system!" Kirsten said.

Asked about her personal motivation for starting her own business, Kirsten said, "I had worked in a travel agency before I had children; however, with the birth of my first child I had to stop working as the day care costs were extravagant and took too much out of my salary to make the job viable. Two years later, technology had progressed to the point where

I was able to start my own travel agency from my home so that I could still be available for my two young children, then an infant and a two-year-old." She elaborated, "Initially it worked quite well, though as my business grew I did find it to be more difficult as I spent more time on my business while still trying to be a full-time mom. I finally did balance this better by setting a work schedule for myself and finding appropriate childcare for my children."

Like all entrepreneurial moms, Kirsten had to strike a balance between work-time and mom-time. "I think it is very important to set a definitive work schedule so that you can balance the time with your children and your work," Kirsten said. "Having a supportive family is also a primary factor in the success of any business, as I often need to rely on my husband to help with household items or childcare when I'm having an unusually busy week." Kirsten went on to add that she also has a housekeeper who comes every other week to assist with the cleaning and that her older children are responsible for cleaning their own rooms and picking up the house daily.

Kirsten also said she is grateful for a supportive husband and family. "I am fortunate to have a great husband who can step in on the weekends or in the evenings if my work is really hectic, though I try to limit working on the weekends," she said. "And I also rely on family occasionally if I am really in a bind."

Although Kirsten works thirty-five to forty hours per week in her business, her children are her main priority. "One of the benefits of owning my own business is being able to have the flexibility to take an hour or two during the day to attend events that are important to my children," Kirsten said. "I make this a priority." And, after being her own boss and enjoying the flexibility it allows, Kirsten said, "Going back to being an employee would be very difficult!"

Laura Zeck created her business, Original Etchings by Laura Zeck, in 2001 prior to becoming a mother. Based in Seattle, Washington, her business offers handmade one-of-a-kind art pieces that each tell a visual story. Laura said her artwork is frequently given as a wedding gift or to celebrate the birth of a child.

An artist all her life, Laura had found herself in a successful, yet fast-paced and high-pressure position working for someone else. It was then that she realized she needed a change and decided to start her own business.

"I think the hardest part was cash flow," Laura said when asked about the obstacles she faced when she first opened her business. "I am lucky," she explained, "to have previously been involved in sales and marketing," adding that she even worked out "trades" when, as she said, "things were running pretty lean."

Although used to hard work, Laura said at times being a business owner has been difficult. "But," she was quick to add, "I am just glad to be putting the effort toward my own business!"

Laura is currently the mother of a fifteen-month-old daughter. To help meet the demands of childcare, Laura uses a nanny on a part-time basis. And to help in her business, Laura uses a part-time assistant. "It is really important to build a support system around yourself," she said.

Asked how she feels about her dual roles as mother and entrepreneur, Laura said, "I never thought I would feel as guilty as I do at times, trying to figure out if I am doing enough of this or that." "But," she added, "I think that comes with the territory of being a mom."

Carrie Wiler, the owner of Scissors Edge Salon in Cocoa, Florida, said being an entrepreneur has enhanced her life. "It's made me a more independent person," she said. The married mother of three children, Carrie has owned her business since 1999. She had worked in the salon business for five years before purchasing an existing business and still sees clients today. She also employs other stylists, nail technicians, and aestheticians in her salon as well.

Juggling her role of entrepreneurial mom has Carrie putting in from forty to fifty hours per week at the salon. Fortunately, however, she has the help of her husband, also an entrepreneur, when it comes to their childcare needs. And to help organize her household, Carrie uses a "chore chart" to have her kids, ages three, nine, and eleven, pitch in around the house.

If Carrie needs to stay home on occasion with an ill child, she said,

"In my business, I'm lucky that I can rearrange my schedule, and most of my clients are pretty understanding."

In Carrie's case, she has found the lack of time and the overwhelming paperwork involved in owning a business to be a drawback because, in her case, she still prefers to see clients. "Nobody cares about your business as much as you do!" Carrie said.

"It took off so fast!" exclaimed **Joy Bocks** as she recalled the swift success of her Florence, South Carolina, business, B & W Motor Company. "I was selling cars, detailing cars, doing paperwork, everything," Joy said. "Good help is hard to find," the married mother of three explained.

Joy's youngest is just three and a half years old. "I pretty much can balance it," Joy said when asked about her dual roles of mother and businesswoman. "On Sunday nights, I plan out what I need to get done that week, both business and personal, using a calendar," Joy explained. "And I always allow myself extra time, with light days on Mondays and Fridays." Joy uses Fridays to catch up on whatever items may have fallen behind schedule during the rest of the week.

Joy uses an in-home day care, allowing her son a home atmosphere with other children. Her caregiver has thirty years of childcare experience, and Joy is pleased with her son's care, which allows her to focus on her daily business.

"The financial part can be stressful on a family," Joy said, referring to starting a new business. "Have a backup plan, a way to get out if necessary," she added.

Joy thinks her business has been successful due to the fact that she is very organized, determined, reliable, and honest. "I like to succeed at anything I do," she said.

And her positive attitude has just led her to take another step into entrepreneurship. Joy has recently opened a second business, L&B Services, which provides labor and demolition services in South Carolina.

Lisa Selman-Holman, owner of Selman-Holman & Associates LLC, of Denton, Texas, started her business in 2004. "My motivation was financial," Lisa said. "I knew I could make more money working for myself."

Lisa felt she could do home-health consulting and education on her own, and she knew the potential revenue. "I was generating a lot of revenue for my employer," Lisa said.

Married and the mother of three children, Lisa had worked in her field for eighteen years. "Home-health consulting is both regulatory and clinical," Lisa explained. "I am both a registered nurse and an attorney."

Lisa sometimes has to travel in her business. Her husband now works for her, and if she has a conference, he goes along to assist. "Sometimes this means that my children travel with us, and sometimes my mother cares for the children," Lisa said.

"I always schedule my clients around my children's activities. I don't miss football games, and I tell my clients I am not available when there is something special going on," Lisa said.

Lisa's husband homeschools their two youngest children, both eight. "My office is in my home," Lisa said. "When Mommy is home, they want to play and go places, whereas I need to set time for work and time for play." She added, "It is difficult to have a getting-off-work time when your office is at home."

"It can be done, but you need help," **Patty Trembley** replied when asked what advice she'd offer to new entrepreneurial moms. Patty opened a breakfast and lunch café in Cocoa Beach, Florida, when her son was four years old. Her café was located in a professional office building on the beach. She owned and managed the business from 1999 to 2001. "I don't think I could have run this kind of business when he was between the first and fourth grades," she explained. "I would have missed too much."

Patty found that being an entrepreneur was definitely more difficult than she had expected. Her mornings started at 4:15 a.m., and she put in ten to twelve hours on the weekends at the café. "I did my shopping and deep cleaning when the café was closed," she said.

Patty credits a supportive husband with helping out with their child-care needs. And because her café served only breakfast and lunch, Patty could pick up her son from preschool on the way home each afternoon. "I missed breakfast with him," Patty said, referring to her son, "but I was able to do other things, like watch his soccer games."

Even though she put in a lot of hours, Patty explained that there were some benefits. "I felt more in control of my time," she said.

Kelly Balcom, owner of KB Creative and Kelly Balcom Designs, is a wife and mother of two young children in Decatur, Georgia. Kelly started her business, a sole proprietorship, in 1999, designing everything from business logos to company Web sites.

At the time she launched her business, Kelly was pregnant with her first child and was working from her home office. After her baby arrived, Kelly scheduled client meetings during the morning hours and used the services of a day care as needed. Then, she explained, she could work on her designs at home, whenever the baby napped.

"Then, with two young children, it got very difficult to work from home!" Kelly said, referring to the arrival of her second child. "It's getting easier now that they are in kindergarten and part-time preschool."

Kelly explained that her decision to be an entrepreneurial mom came about because she could design her own products and still bring in an income and not be on a client-determined deadline. "I thought if I could create my own products, then I could design whenever a creative thought came to mind," Kelly said.

Tana Baumler, along with two good friends, bought the Maltby Café in Maltby, Washington, in 1988 after going there for breakfast themselves many times. Tana, a wife and the mother of a two-year-old and a five-year old at the time, had always wanted to own a restaurant. She had previous experience working in a restaurant and as a baker.

Fortunately for Tana, she had the support of her husband and her family. "You make it work," she said. "It means a lot of long hours and not a lot of sleep!" Tana said she was overwhelmed by the amount of hours involved in running a business. "But," she added, "success motivates you!"

Tana is from a large family and had a very supportive mother and father who were able to visit for several months every year, helping out with the children, she said. Also, Tana explained, her friend had a day care where she could take her children if needed.

Being an entrepreneur has "absolutely enhanced" Tana's family's life. "Through my restaurant family," she explained, "our kids have seen the cycle of life, from births to marriages." Tana herself has been married for twenty-nine years, and just became a proud grandmother for the first time.

Faith plays a large part in Tana's life. Her business has fifty-four employees, which she refers to as a mini-ministry, with a lot of single parents and youth. "As a Christian, I look at it like they're under my wing for the moment and I am to help shape them. Single moms were led our direction for a reason, as a place of rest and healing," she said. Tana explained, "The restaurant had a big impact on my children; the restaurant people are our extended family."

I hope the glimpses of themselves these entrepreneurial moms have shared with you will show you the good and the bad, the ups and the downs to be expected if you become an entrepreneurial mom yourself. I hope you take away that it all comes down to choices. Choices about what is most important to you; choices about what you want to teach your children; choices about the opportunities you want to offer your family. There is no right or wrong answer about whether to run your own business or stay home with your children. Every mom questions herself at some time, but you have to make a choice, and once you've made a decision, stick with it. (A very wise woman once gave me that advice. She was, in fact, a mother. To be precise, she was *my* mother.)

Setting Up Your Business

In 1992, when I decided to start my own business, I must admit that it was an overwhelming and at times lonely feeling, knowing I had to navigate uncharted waters. There were so many considerations before I could even open my doors for business! I tried, unsuccessfully, to find a road map to lead me through the snarl of paperwork and questions I faced.

There were so many areas to be addressed! *Do I incorporate? What type of corporation is right for me? What kind of insurance coverage do I need? How do I find an office space? How do I negotiate a commercial lease? How do I set up accounts with vendors? What should I do since I don't have established credit for my new business? Should I extend credit to my own customers? What happens if my customers don't pay me?* Whew! The questions whirled around in my head! (Frankly, I think this flood of questions may be the reason many people don't get any farther than the "idea phase" for starting their own business!)

Because you are already a busy mom, you need to find information fast that will allow you to move with ease through the maze of paperwork and legal requirements in front of you.

Following is some the information that I would have found helpful as I began to set up my new business. Whether you are a male or a female, married or single, old or young, you will encounter the same initial legalities and considerations as you set up your new business.

The information in this chapter is not meant to be exhaustive, but these are suggestions you may wish to consider based on my experience. I would recommend that you consult both an attorney and an accountant with any questions that may arise during the initial set-up phase of your business.

Market Research

Market research is a very broad area that is difficult to get into in general terms. Nonetheless, it is a critical process for all types of businesses, whether they offer products or services.

Before taking the big plunge into entrepreneurship, familiarize yourself with your market. What types of customers do you want to attract? What is the average age of your ideal customer? Are they male, female, or will both men and women use your product or service? What is the income level of your target market? How much are they willing to pay for what you're selling? Who are your direct competitors? Can you improve upon your product or service to make it more attractive? These are just some of the questions for which you'll want to seek answers. The answers will help you in positioning your product or service, pricing it, and presenting it to your market.

Don't be afraid to ask questions! And be prepared for some negative feedback. Wouldn't you rather get it now, while you can still improve upon your product or service? People love to express their opinions, good and bad. Compile your feedback now; you can sort it out later, and decide how to use it.

Have you ever driven by a store and thought, "What were they thinking when they put *that* store in *this* neighborhood?" We've all seen businesses come and go, and usually they go because their owner didn't do their homework first. Many great ideas have gone to waste simply because they weren't marketed correctly or they were offered to the wrong group of people or positioned incorrectly. For instance, you wouldn't open a tractor supply company in Manhattan, a nightclub in the middle of an Amish community, or a baby boutique in a retirement community.

Doing your research is simpler than it sounds. The depth of your research will depend on you and what your business is offering. Start by creating a survey listing questions pertinent to your business. For instance, if you will build and service swimming pools, you'll want to know the age of the homes in your targeted geographic area; the size of the houses; the size of the lot the houses occupy; the income levels of your survey participants; whether they currently have a pool (for which they need chemicals or better yet, a monthly service); if they plan on building or resurfacing their pool within the next year; how much they would be willing to pay for a monthly service; the size of the pool they'd like to build and how much they'd expect to pay for its construction; whether or not they have children in their home (families are more likely to use a pool—plus if they have young children, they'll need a security fence or pool alarm); and finally, if you can contact them later regarding your business. Your county offices may be able to provide some of the information you seek, such as the ages of homes in various subdivisions; new residents building in your area; recent construction permits; and the number of similar companies already in business in your area.

If you've created a line of baby products, you'll want to find out the ages of the people in your geographic area (are they of child-bearing age or are they senior citizens?); the ages of their children; whether they plan on having more children; their income level; where they currently buy similar products; how much they'd be willing to pay for your products. You could also check with the area school board office, which could provide the number of schools, their enrollment, and the ages of the students. (Lots of schools mean younger families with a likelihood of infants whose parents could use your products.)

Also, if possible, it would be helpful to show a sample of your product to your survey participants. Obviously, if you are mailing your surveys this wouldn't work, but if you could arrange to personally administer the surveys at a church, a local park, or your local library, you could display your product.

Don't be deflated if you receive negative responses or find out that your business may not work in the area where your survey respondents live. Your data may tell you that it's better to position your business in a different area or possibly offer your product or service via the Internet, where you can reach a broader market.

If this process seems like more than you want to tackle yourself, there are firms that, for a fee, provide in-depth demographics and viability studies for your proposed business. If you hire a firm to do the homework for you, be specific as to your expectations and your intentions, so you won't end up paying for useless information.

The information you collect will be invaluable in determining where to open your business and how to best reach your customers. The time you spend on this phase will save you time and money later!

Naming Your "Baby"

By now you have decided on the type of business you wish to own and operate, and chances are you've played around with a few names for the business. Before settling on a name, give this area careful consideration! One of the most important tasks in starting your new business is selecting its name. Just as you put much thought into naming your children, you will want to do the same when naming your business!

It is your responsibility to ensure the name is not already in use, currently registered, or trademarked by another company. One of the ways to check this is to contact your state attorney's office and ask for a "name search." You can do this via telephone or by using the Internet. Check with your attorney for laws as they apply to your state before settling on a business name. (It is *very* expensive to find out later that you must change your business name because you have infringed on the rights of another!)

Your business name should be simple, catchy, and easily remembered. It should also be easy to spell so people can locate it in the phone book with ease. The name should have a positive connotation so when your business name is used in conversation it leaves people with a good impression and high expectations.

Keep the name short, but descriptive. Let people know what your business offers. For instance a sign that reads "JACKIE'S" tells passersby absolutely nothing about the business. Yet, a sign that reads "JACKIE'S FINE INTERIORS & DECORATING" lets people know instantly what to expect of the business. Similarly, a business called Classy Salon may not bring in as many customers as one called Classy Hair, Nails, & Day Spa, even though both may offer the same services. In an instant, motorists should receive a snapshot of the services a business offers from its sign. So, the more descriptive yet succinct you can be when naming your business, the better. Another important tip to remember when ordering the sign for your business is to add your phone number. If a potential customer does not have time to stop in, they can call for information or for an appointment if they have your phone number. (And, we busy moms can all relate to driving a minivan full of kids while running errands and not having time to make even one more stop.) Personally, I am grateful to businesses that list phone numbers, so I can grab my cell phone and schedule my car alignment or a hair appointment while driving the kids to basketball practice. If there's one thing all moms do well, it's multitasking.

When selecting your business name, keep in mind possible expansion in your business. Don't box yourself in, limiting yourself later. Just because today you offer custom-designed stationery, who's to say that next year you won't want to also carry hand-painted collectibles and scented candles? If you name your business Sally's Stationery, it will be hard to market your other items later. But if you plan ahead and use a broader name, like Sally's Stationery & Gifts, you will have more latitude should you decide to expand your business and offer a broader range of items.

Corporations

Anyone can incorporate a business. There are many reasons for incorporating, but one of the most common is to create an entity separate from oneself. Your new corporation will be treated as a separate being, with assets and liabilities of its own. There are many different types of corporations. Here are a few:

GENERAL CORPORATION

This is the most common type of corporation. It is a separate entity and is owned by stockholders. A general corporation can have an unlimited number of stockholders. The stockholders' personal liability is limited to the amount of the investment they have in the corporation. With a general corporation, it is easier to raise capital through the sale of stock, should the need arise. This type of corporation is more expensive to form, however, due to the legal formalities.

CLOSE CORPORATION

Check with your individual state to see if it recognizes this type of corporation. Usually, a close corporation is limited to fifty stockholders. This type of corporation is suited more to a group of people who will own the corporation, with only some of these people actively involved in running the business.

S CORPORATION

An S corporation is not really a different type of corporation, but rather a special designation recognized by the IRS for certain corporations. This type of corporation is desirable for many small business owners due to the tax advantages it offers. The biggest advantage of this type of corporation is that it will avoid "double taxation" of the income (or loss) of a business. This is because the company's income (or loss) is reflected in the personal tax returns of the shareholders. To be considered for this special designation, your corporation must meet specific guidelines. Meet with your accountant for a full disclosure of these guidelines.

LIMITED LIABILITY COMPANY OR LLC

Many people think LLCs offer a great alternative to both corporations and partnerships because they combine the advantages of both entities. With an LLC, business owners can enjoy corporate liability protection plus some tax advantages, such as the protection of personal assets from business debt. As with an S corporation, the profits (or losses) of the company will be reflected in the personal tax returns of the business owner. Some states will require at least two members to form an LLC. Check with your state for specifics involved in forming an LLC.

Because you are a mom, with children and a family to protect, it is highly advisable to form some type of a corporation, or separate entity,

THE ENTREPRENEURIAL MOM

from which to conduct business. Check with your attorney or another trusted adviser about the type of corporation that is right for you. This is something you should do right away!

Your Company Identification Numbers

Just like you have a personal Social Security number issued by the government, your business will have a number identifying it also. This number is called an FEI number or federal employer identification number. Obtain this number by contacting the Internal Revenue Service either by telephone or via the Internet. Provide the requested information, and you will be assigned a number identifying your new business. And voilà! a new taxpayer is born to the U.S. government and your paperwork begins!

If your business is required to collect state sales tax, contact the local tax collector's office to obtain information about registering as a new business. You will be assigned yet another number by your state for the purpose of state tax collection and a representative will provide information about how and when to collect and pay your state taxes. If you are unsure of your obligation to collect or pay state tax, contact your local tax collector's office for information about compliance.

If you have employees, you must register your business with your state's unemployment insurance division, which is located in the state offices of the Department of Labor. Your business will be assigned yet another number, and you will be required to file reports and make payments to your state. Your state will assign a percentage rate from which to calculate amounts due. This rate is based on payroll amounts and later also on any unemployment compensation claims made by former employees of your business.

Also, contact your state to inquire about workers' compensation requirements for your business. They vary, not only by state, but also by industry in each state. In some states, companies with fewer than four employees are not required to carry workers' compensation insurance coverage, although you still have the option to carry the coverage if you wish to do so. If you must carry the coverage, sometimes, as an officer of your corporation, you can exempt yourself, thereby saving on your premiums. Definitely explore this area prior to hiring employees for your new business, so your business will be in compliance with your state's laws.

The Assurance of Insurance

Your next big consideration should be insurance. As a mom, it is your natural instinct to provide protection for your family. Continue to protect your family by obtaining the insurance that is best for you and your circumstances.

There are many types of insurance available today. I have listed some of the types you may wish to consider for your business, but this section is by no means meant to be comprehensive.

GENERAL OR EMPLOYER'S LIABILITY INSURANCE

This type of insurance will offer protection to you if someone is injured or suffers a loss due to the result of an action by you or an employee of your business. Do not skimp on this insurance. Purchase as much coverage as you can afford! And, if you will employ subcontractors in your business, ensure that they, too, carry this insurance. Have them provide you with a Certificate of Insurance, listing your business as the certificate holder. If they do not carry this insurance, then they are working under your company's insurance, which leads to exposure for your company. (And, without their own insurance, they are not recognized as a true subcontractor.)

WORKERS' COMPENSATION INSURANCE

This is insurance that will provide for compensation to your employees if they are injured on the job. Check with your state for the rules of workers' compensation, as they apply to your specific industry.

AUTOMOBILE INSURANCE

Just like with your personal vehicle, you will want automobile insurance for any vehicles owned by your company or driven by your employees. In order to get the best insurance rate for auto insurance, check the driving backgrounds of potential employees. The fewer accumulated points a driver has against his license, the lower the cost of insurance for that driver.

LIFE INSURANCE

If you are the owner of a small business, it may be advisable for you to protect your family in the event of your death, as they will suddenly be left without your income. There are many factors to consider when purchasing life insurance. Contact a trusted insurance salesperson for this information, as there are several different types of life insurance available.

DISABILITY INSURANCE

This type of insurance will be important should you become incapacitated and unable to perform the usual duties of running your business. The policy would be structured to pay you during the period you are unable to work.

KEY PERSON INSURANCE

Key Person Insurance provides coverage when a person who is "key" to your business is unable to perform his job due to disability or even death. The policy provides for the financial loss your company suffers as a result of the loss of this individual's services.

PRODUCT LIABILITY INSURANCE

In the event that you sell a product to a consumer who is subseqently injured by the product, the consumer could bring suit against your company, as well as the product's manufacturer. Consult your attorney as to your exposure in this area.

LOSS-OF-BUSINESS INSURANCE

This insurance provides for compensation should your business be unable to operate due to physical damage to the business as a result of flood, fire, etc. Typically, acts of war are not included in areas of coverage for loss-of-business insurance. Your sales receipts will be used to compute the amount of this insurance coverage you need.

Again, please note that the aforementioned examples of insurance coverage are only some of the types of insurance for you to consider as a new entrepreneur. It is highly advisable that you explore all options of insurance coverage available to you. When you are an entrepreneurial mom, it is so important to protect yourself in all areas of both your business and personal life.

Finding a Location for Your Business

There are many considerations when it comes to finding a location for your business. And the rent is only one of them. If your business will depend on in-store sales, chances are you'll need a highly visible, heavily traveled location. Unfortunately, this usually means you will pay a higher rental amount, because those types of spaces are more desirable and, therefore, more costly. But if you do not need a highly visible location, you have many more options available to you. You may be able to find office space in a business park, or a plaza that is tucked away from the traffic. The rents in these more out-of-the-way places are generally less. If you are looking for a retail space in a mall, the price per square foot will vary based on your location and the current economic conditions, but rent or lease costs will most likely be higher than elsewhere.

In selecting a location, also consider the convenience of the office to your home. After all, you are the most important employee of your business, and you will still be a mom when your business opens, with all of the usual "mom responsibilities." If you can place your office within close proximity to your home and, if possible, also to your kids' school, it will be a great time-saver later!

As an entrepreneurial mom, you will find that you will perform your mom duties *and* your business duties every day, so make it convenient to travel between your home, your office, and your children's school! There have been countless times that I have gone into the office for a couple of hours, then slipped out to attend my daughter's spelling bee and run back to the office after it was over; also, I have dropped my son off at basketball practice and used that hour to run by my office and catch up on paperwork before I picked him up after practice.

So, give the location of your business some serious thought! Make it convenient to you, your company's most important employee!

Negotiating a Business Lease

First, do not be intimidated by this process! That landlord wants you as badly as you want his office space! If the rental space you are considering is not up to par, request that the landlord make necessary repairs before the term of your lease begins. In many instances a commercial lease provides for CAM or "common area maintenance" fees, which are added into your rental amount. Try to negotiate a fixed amount and a cap on these fees. Also, depending upon your state's sales tax laws, the rental amount you pay may be taxable.

Take a few minutes to talk with other tenants who lease from your prospective landlord. They will be happy to give you feedback, be it good or bad!

Walk around and look at the condition of the building and the grounds. Are they maintained? Are they clean? Also, visit the building at night, after dark. Are there working pole lights or floodlights in the parking lot? Remember, you may be at your office after dark at times, and your safety is a priority.

Before signing a lease, check with local, city, or county zoning offices to ensure that your particular business will be approved to operate within their parameters.

For obvious reasons, it would be to your benefit to insert a clause in your lease prohibiting your landlord from leasing space to a business that might be in direct competition with yours. This is a matter of ethics and good business, and most landlords are willing to provide this assurance to their tenants in writing.

Have the lease list your business name as the lessee. When you sign the lease, sign it as a representative of your corporation, using your official title, which will most likely be "President" (Example: *Sally Smith, President*). Again, you are obligating your corporation, and not yourself! (And you are protecting yourself and your family, should it become necessary for the landlord to enforce the lease.)

It is advisable to decline to date the lease or take possession of the property until any necessary repairs or alterations have been performed, as agreed upon by the landlord. Your rental period should commence on the date the property is delivered in the promised condition by the landlord.

Know Your Banker

As a mom, you've probably already found out how important relationships can be. Relationships with trusted neighbors; relationships with your children's caregiver; relationships with your children's teachers; even the relationships your children form between friends. Forming relationships with trusted individuals is also key to the success of your new business.

If you already have personal bank accounts, a mortgage, a car loan, or maybe a boat loan with a local bank, stay with that bank, at least for now, when setting up your business banking. At least you have some established history with your current bank and have, hopefully, created a positive track record for yourself.

When opening your business bank account, you will need to provide certain documentation to your banker. Take along photocopies of your corporate papers, showing the corporation as an entity separate from yourself. Take with you the federal employer identification number assigned to your business by the IRS. And also take your personal driver's license. If another individual, such as your spouse, a business partner, or an employee will be a signer on the account, that person will also be required to sign the original signature card, which is maintained in the branch where you open your business account. This person need not be present on the day you open the account, but can stop in at a later date and complete the signature card if you leave instructions to do so.

Consider requiring two signatures for checks over a certain amount. For example, you may allow your bookkeeper to sign checks under $5,000, but require your signature for checks over that amount or require both signatures on any checks over that amount.

By remaining with the same bank where you have personally banked in the past, you will establish a reputation and a continued history with that financial institution. This may be important to you at a later date, should it be necessary for your business to obtain a business loan or a business line of credit.

But don't assume that just because your money is in their bank, the employees know you. Take the time to chat with your bankers and develop relationships. You'll be glad you did when, from time to time, you need a hold removed from a customer's check early or you need some other courtesy extended.

If your bank is not already offering the most attractive and competitive fees, *ask* for them! Negotiate the best rates possible for your business. Most banks today are happy to accommodate business customers in order to keep their patronage. Many bankers will actually waive some of their standard fees and the cost of business checks for their customers.

Chances are that your bank even offers online business banking, which is extremely convenient, especially for the busy entrepreneurial mom. With online banking, you can access your accounts anytime, day or night, simply by logging on to your computer. You can even pay your bills online and set up recurring payments, such as rent, to be debited from your bank account on a scheduled day each month.

If your business will accept credit cards as a form of customer payment, your bank can set this up for you, although be sure to check their processing rates. For more information on accepting credit cards from your customers, ask your bank about their merchant services program and fees. A designated representative will be assigned to help you. A bit of advice in this area: Shop around! There are many merchant services companies, all offering different rates and services and all eager for new business. Your rate will be based on the average amount of sales you will process, and a rate of even half a percentage point can add up to a lot of money over a twelve-month period. You will need the equipment on which to accept credit-card charges as well. This can be leased or purchased from your merchant services vendor. Your credit card machine will be set up in your office and connected through your telephone line, most likely. Or, some companies provide for access through your computer. A representative from the merchant services company will most likely come out to set this up and go over procedures with you if you are new to the process. It's very simple, and telephone assistance is always available should you have any questions or problems. Be aware that even though you sign on with a merchant services company, you have the right to shop their rates and move your business if you find a better deal elsewhere. Remember: It's not just about making money, but about saving the money you make!

A Business Plan

If you're like most entrepreneurial moms I know, your business plan is neatly organized in your own head, rather than on paper. Between raising your kids and running your household, you've compiled all the details and plans for your own business. While driving the car pool with five chattering eight-year-olds in the back of your SUV, you've come up with lots of great ideas about how to make your business work. Well, take the time to commit this information to paper, right now, before you get too immersed in the day-to-day particulars of running your business to slow down and "steer it." Even if you don't need a business plan to obtain financing or start-up capital from a lender, you do need a plan for your own direction and reinforcement, in order to keep yourself on track.

The term *business plan* sounds formal and possibly even intimidating to some people. You will be surprised at how simple it is to construct a business plan once you begin. Basically, you will answer several questions: What? Where? To whom? and How?

Begin with the name of your business. Next, write a description of your business, noting the goods and/or services it will provide. List the location from which your business will operate. Identify your customer base, no matter how broad. Write down the goals you have for your business and a timeline in which to achieve these objectives. Ask yourself many questions during this process: How do you intend to market? What is your marketing budget? How does your business compare to similar businesses in your area? Is there any unique value to your business that makes it stand apart from similar businesses? How much start-up capital do you have? Do you have a second source for additional monies if needed?

Your business plan can be informal, unless, of course, it is to be presented to a lender or investors. But in any case, you must have a plan!

Refer to it often in order to stay on course, keeping your goals in sight. And be aware that most likely you will revise your business plan several times as your business evolves. That's fine! It means your business is moving ahead and that you are thinking and planning. Revision can be a good thing. In business, you'll find that you never want to stand still. Those who stand still get run over by the pack!

Setting Up Vendors and Vendor Accounts

Depending on the nature of your business, you may already have vendor contacts. For instance, if you've been making pottery, you've ordered supplies for years. If you now own a hair salon, you may have worked in one previously, renting your station and ordering your own products; therefore, you have vendor contacts already. If so, it will be easy to notify them of your new, retail location. Most sales reps from your vendor and supply companies will be eager to assist you in your grand opening. Some will even offer free samples and promotional items, hoping to get shelf space or a display location in your shop. Other reps will be generous with their time, perhaps even offering to assist in setting up your showroom and displays. And, as a busy entrepreneurial mom, you will want to accept all offers of assistance!

If you do not already have relationships with vendors and suppliers in your industry, you must establish your business with them. This means establishing a history and creditworthiness for your business. The thing you will find is that some companies won't be willing to extend credit because your business has no credit history yet. And how can you build a credit history if no one wants to extend you credit?

Be prepared to offer some options and suggestions if the credit departments of your prospective vendors turn you down for an open credit account. First, you can offer to sign a personal guaranty, whereby you will be personally liable for any debt incurred by your company. Another option is to offer to allow the vendor to keep a credit card on file with a signed consent that your credit card is to be charged in the event your company fails to pay its debt. Another possible solution is to offer to provide the vendor with a reserve deposit of funds that can be applied against an unpaid debt if that should become necessary. And finally, if the vendor does not agree to cooperate with any of your creative credit options, you can request to be a COD (cash on delivery) Account or CBD (cash before delivery) Account. If you opt for either of these last two options, ask for a discount for early payment with these terms that are obviously favorable to the vendor. Depending on the size of an invoice, it is not unreasonable to request a 5 to 8 percent discount on COD and CBD orders. At the end of a year, this small percentage really adds up! Also ask your vendor if there is any incentive or discount to group your orders together and ship items only once or twice a month. With fluctuating fuel prices, many vendors are willing to offer incentives if they can send fewer shipments and group orders together, thereby saving them money in their distribution costs.

As a mom, you've been clipping coupons and looking for discounts in the past, and now as an entrepreneurial mom, you need to apply the same money-saving strategies and thinking to your business. Especially during slow times, if you're not making money, you should be saving money!

Hiring Employees

When you are ready to hire your first employee, there are many things to consider. First, be prepared to put some time and effort into finding the right person to fill your position. As a busy entrepreneurial mom, you don't have time to perform this step twice!

First, before you begin the search for your first employee, acquaint yourself with the federal antidiscrimination laws as they pertain to hiring. Below are some of the laws that prohibit job discrimination in the United States:

- Equal Pay Act of 1963. This law ensures that men and women who perform the equal work are not discriminated against based on their gender.

- Civil Rights Act of 1964, Title VII. Prohibits discrimination due to race, color, religion, sex, or national origin.

- Age Discrimination in Employment of 1967. This was written to protect people forty years of age or older from being discriminated against due to their age.

- Americans with Disabilities Act of 1990, Titles I and V. Prohibits discrimination against individuals who are qualified, yet disabled, and who work in the private sector.

- Civil Rights Act of 1991. Among other things, this law provides for monetary damages to be awarded in cases of intentional employment discrimination.

The U.S. Equal Employment Opportunity Commission (EEOC) enforces these laws. For more information or clarification on the laws or for information on employment regulations and practices, contact the EEOC. For information about the antidiscrimination laws in your state, contact your state's labor department.

Depending on the type of position for which you are hiring, there are several ways to begin your search. If you are looking for a general office person to help out in your new business, you may find the simplest and least expensive method is to advertise your opening in your local newspaper. If, however, you are looking for a more skilled or technical person, you will have better results going through an employment agency or job placement service. Some people even find their employees by going to the many online sites on the Internet where applicants post their résumés and qualifications.

Because time is at a premium, simplify your interview process from the start by asking applicants to send their résumés to you before you even consider scheduling an interview. This will allow you to review the résumés and then schedule interviews with people whose experience and personal goals most closely fit your immediate needs. Basically, it will weed out those applicants you definitely don't want, saving you hours of time just going through the interview motions with each applicant.

Sometimes, just letting your applicant talk will tell you all you need to know in a single sentence. Once, while interviewing for a full-time sales position in our showroom, an applicant explained that she wanted a job that allowed her "time to study" for her college classes (interview over!). Several years ago, I was interviewing a man for a flooring installer's job with my company, explaining to him that we like to start our day early. He interrupted me to let me know he couldn't be at work until 9:30 on any given day, due to the fact that he had to "stop by the methadone clinic first thing every morning" (interview over!).

If you are hiring someone for an office position, don't waver on your requirements of this person. It will be you who suffers in the end if your office is not managed up to your standards. But go into your search fully aware that the best person may not always have the most experience. You would be far better off hiring a positive, motivated team player who will put forth great initiative, rather than the quiet clock-watcher whose greatest accomplishment is her rapid typing speed. The positive, motivated applicant will be willing to learn, if given the opportunity.

For the past several years, I have been fortunate to have a terrific office manager working for me. She stays on top of our orders, is great with our customers, handles our subcontractors with ease, and takes care of all the "little details" that I am too busy to handle. Because she is also the mother of three children, I have no problem being flexible if she needs time off for a field trip or has to stay home on occasion with a sick child. I am certain it is because I, too, am a working mother that I understand her situation. But because I am willing to be flexible with her at times, she, in turn, gives me 110 percent and goes the extra mile for me and my business.

After narrowing your options to several qualified applicants, take the time to check their references. Many times, previous employers will decline altogether to give a reference and may only verify dates of employment. But remember, you can ask the previous employer if they would rehire the individual themselves if given the opportunity. Their answer, whether positive or negative, may tell you what you want to know!

I have also preferred to check my applicants' criminal history when considering a new hire. You can do this on the Internet and have results back in minutes, often for as little as $19, a small price to pay to protect yourself, your customers, and the good name of your business!

When you have decided on your new hire, make it clear that you are offering them the position on a trial basis. On their first day of work, present your new employee with a typed, formal job description, in which their responsibilities are clearly outlined. Have the new employee sign it after you've discussed it thoroughly, and give the employee his own copy to keep. As an employer, you are required to have all employees sign specific forms upon their hire. The W-4 form allows the new employee to specify the number of dependents they wish to claim. You will need this form in order to prepare your new employee's payroll. Also, if your state has a withholding tax, you are required to have the employee fill out a WH-4 state withholding form as well.

The I-9 form was created to enable employers to verify the employment eligibility of their new hires. All employees hired after November 6, 1986, are required to complete an I-9 form upon hire. As an employer, it is your responsibility to inspect your new employees' documents verifying their identity and their eligibility to work in the United States. Upon examining the documents, you must note the title of the verification document viewed, the document number, and the document's expiration date, if any. It is your responsibility to have a copy of a completed I-9 form on file for each employee of your business. For more information about the I-9 form, contact the Immigration & Naturalization Service to request the INS Handbook, Form M-274.

If your business or your employee leasing company offers direct deposit of employees' paychecks, your new employee will fill out forms with their bank account information as well. If your employee will be entitled to health insurance (after their probationary period), paid sick leave, or vacation time, you may choose to wait until the end of his trial period before formally going over these areas.

As your new employee begins his probationary period, you must remember that working directly for an entrepreneur like yourself is entirely different from working for a large company with many employees. In all fairness to your new employee, you should be willing to give him time to adjust to the new dynamics of this employment.

Take time when explaining your office procedures. Spend extra time when introducing your employee to your customer base and the way in which your customers are to be handled. Your customers should receive the same treatment from all employees in your business. Make sure your new employee is keenly aware of the value you place on your customers, so he can model your mind-set when dealing with your customers.

During your employee's probationary period, give him feedback as to his performance. When your employee's performance is top-notch, let him know. If there is something you'd like done differently, simply say so. Many times, a great employee is lost simply due to poor communication.

Most likely, you will know before his trial period is over if your new employee should be a permanent hire. You will observe how well he fits into your workplace environment, you will test his ability (or inability) to problem-solve, you will witness his interaction with your customers; and you will see his overall level of initiative. If you decide to make your employee permanent, let him know why you've made your decision, citing his positive performance. Also, if your business structure allows, it may be wise to tie his earnings to a measurable scale, such as sales, if he will be dealing with your customers. If you are able to offer even a small bonus, over and above his salary, based on the company's performance— do it! You will be building a team, and, in the end, it will be you, the business owner, who wins! Your employee will feel like a valued and vital team member, your customers will be well cared for, and you will not be the only one working toward the success of your business!

Employee Leasing Programs

Many businesses, both large and small, have turned to employee leasing to handle their human resources needs. Employee leasing companies charge fees to businesses to handle the "paper shuffle" associated with employees. This includes payroll services, benefits management, tax compliances, workers' compensation insurance, and risk management.

Employee leasing companies handle businesses that have thousands of employees or just one employee. Rates and services will vary.

Signs for Your Vehicle

Use your vehicle as another means of advertising! For less than $100, you can have a pair of tasteful magnetic advertising signs made. As you drive to and from appointments or even on personal errands, your vehicle will advertise your business. But a word of caution, ladies: You are now a woman driving around with your phone number printed on the door of your vehicle. Be careful! When you get a call to meet with a customer in their home, take a second person with you for your personal safety. Also, leave a daily log of appointments with another person, such as your office assistant. This way, if you find yourself in a compromising or even dangerous situation, someone will know where to find you.

I have never, in more than fifteen years, had my personal safety jeopardized, but I have been in uncomfortable situations as a woman. My job takes me into people's homes, and, in nearly all instances, my customers are strangers to me. I always telephone or radio my office, or sometimes my husband, in front of the customer, advising of my location and the time I expect to be "available for my next appointment." While this is not a foolproof method of ensuring my safety, it is at least a deterrent if a customer has ill intentions.

It is unfortunate that we even must consider the possibility of harm coming to us in the course of our daily business dealings. But it is a fact of life, and, as a woman, I caution you to take precautions and use safety measures!

Tracking Your Advertising Results

As customers begin visiting your business, ask each of them how they heard about you. Was it the print ad you ran in Sunday's newspaper? Did they see your press release? Did their friend receive one of your personal letters? Was your vehicle spotted around town with your company's sign? Or did they just happen by and see the sign above your business? It is imperative, especially in the early stages of your business, that you track your leads. Know where your traffic comes from and which method of advertising is working for you. This information will enable you to spend your advertising dollars where they are getting the best results. But don't be too hasty in dropping a certain advertising method. Give it a chance to work. A good benchmark is to run an ad at least three times before deciding if it's working or not. Keep a log indicating your customers' responses to queries about how they heard of your business. After a while, your log will provide you with invaluable information as to which advertising methods work best.

Using Your Existing Customer Base

After you've completed a sale with a customer, never assume you are finished with that customer. If they were pleased with your service, they will likely use you again or they will become a form of free advertising for you. After you complete a transaction with each customer, take the time to send a thank-you note, handwritten of course, expressing your gratitude for the trust they placed in your business.

Keep a customer log, complete with customers' names, addresses, and telephone numbers. On special occasions such as the holidays, send your customers cards wishing them the best for the season.

In my business, we send Christmas cards to our customers and our vendors every year, wishing them a joyous holiday season. (Because there are many religions today, I found that "holiday" cards were preferable, and would be appreciated by everyone.) We also send Thanksgiving cards to our customers expressing our gratitude for their patronage. I found that my customers were so thrilled that we took the time to say "Thanks" at Thanksgiving that many of them actually called to say so! And our cards were always hand-signed by me, the owner, and each carried a personal note inside. Who among us doesn't have time for a little gratitude?

Your customer list will also come in handy many times throughout the year as you strive to keep your business name in front of your customers. You can do this with postcards announcing new products or services, letters announcing new employees, newsletters about things happening in your industry that might impact your customers, advertisements, and invitations to stop by your shop and see your newest items. Previous customers are an excellent source of new business by way of referrals. Keep the channels of communication open with your customers as you grow your business!

Tracking Your Profit

To obtain an overview of how your business is doing, you need to measure its progress. In the beginning stages of your business, you will want to do this on a monthly basis, so you can adjust quickly if necessary.

You can monitor your profit (or loss) through the usage of a P&L (profit and loss) report. Basically, this report will show the amount of your pretax sales, less how much it cost you to get those sales, less your fixed expenses and liabilities. What's left will be your profit (or loss) each month.

If you are using a computerized accounting program, you can generate your P&L report in seconds. The information is derived from the invoices you've already created and the checks you've already written that have been assigned to specific accounts.

By studying the numbers, you will see if sales need to go up or expenses need to come down. Maybe your office is "top-heavy" and having two office people is draining your business financially. Perhaps you need to look to your vendors for better prices or shipping discounts to cut expenses. Or, possibly, you just need to work even harder to get your sales numbers up.

All businesses, big or small, live and die by their numbers. If you want to be a successful entrepreneur, use your data to run your company.

Collecting Your Money

First, let me say that if you are in a business where you do not have to carry an accounts receivable, you are ahead of the game already and can skip this section! Collecting the monies owed your company can be tricky and at times even perilous to the life of your business.

If you do carry an accounts receivable, you probably have commercial or business customers. Frequently the home offices of your customers will even be located in another state. Most businesses to whom you have extended credit had every intention of paying you for your goods and services at the time they received them. But, as the debt grows older, it is more difficult to collect. Your product is not so new anymore, your service is not as fresh in the minds of those who requested it. And the older the invoice gets, the less likely you are to collect payment for it. So, you must act swiftly!

The old adage is true: "The squeaky wheel gets the grease." And because you may wish to continue to do business with your customer in the future, you will find that you must tread lightly as you begin to "squeak."

It is prudent to request a credit application from your potential customer prior to opening an account for them. (Technically, you will be letting them use your money, so you have a right to look at their creditworthiness.) Check out their credit references. Ask about their payment history. You may find that your potential customer does not pay as agreed in thirty days, but always pays within forty-five days. This is valuable information to you. Possibly when pricing your products and services, you may wish to build in a late-payment factor to the price you offer your customer. Also, you will be able to make an informed decision as to whether you wish to carry this customer past your normal payment terms, or if you'd rather not extend them payment terms.

Request banking information on the credit application also. Customers will likely provide this to you up front, and if you must go to court later seeking payment, it is easier to garnish a bank account if you can find it. If you choose to extend credit to a customer, have a written agreement as to your payment terms and your remedy to obtain payment should the customer fail to pay you. Make clear any charges that will be passed on to the customer as a result of their late payment. If your business will provide improvements to a property, you may be required to send a Notice to Owner or Notice of Commencement form to the property's owner stating when work will commence and that the owner is being obligated by his representatives to pay you for your services. If you will place a lien on a property for unpaid invoices for improvements, state this. If you will litigate to collect any unpaid amounts, clearly state this, noting that venue will be in your county and that you also will collect all applicable attorney and collection fees. (Remember, a property's owner or management company may be outside your state, but you don't want to have to travel to litigate your claim. Usually a venue is in the same county as the subject property you service. Keep it simple.)

Also be clear about your company's return policy or if every sale is final. If you will apply payments to the oldest invoices on an account first, state this. Be specific about the credit limit you will set for your customer. Have this agreement signed by an authorized representative of your customer's company and have the agreement witnessed by another party. Provide a copy of the agreement to the customer and keep the original for your file. (*Note:* This is an area in which I suggest you seek the specific advice of an attorney who can guide you and protect your interests fully. The aforementioned points are only suggested guidelines, some of which I learned about the hard way over the years.)

Once you open accounts for your customers, the nail-biting begins! You will be using your credit with your vendors to procure materials or products that you, in turn, will sell to your customers, who will charge their purchases to the accounts they've opened with you. A word of caution here: Closely monitor your accounts receivable. Watch each customer's activity. (Even if you employ a bookkeeper, make it your business to watch your accounts receivable. No one cares about your company as much as you do!) If a customer nears their credit limit quickly and they are still within their payment terms, this could mean several things. First, possibly their credit limit has been set too low as they will do a larger volume of business with you than you had expected. If they make timely payments, this is great news. Or, are they jamming their credit limit quickly, only to come back and ask for a higher limit because they are still within their payment terms? In which case, you may be along for an expensive ride!

I got a lightning-fast education many years ago as a new entrepreneur. I had many commercial accounts to whom I was selling materials. Some accounts were better payers than others. The sales were going up, up, up. Great! Their account balances were going up, up, up. Also, great! I expected plenty of checks in my mailbox soon. My indebtedness to my suppliers was also going up, up, up. Very scary! Especially when a bulk of the customers' invoices came due and their checks were not showing up as I had expected. Fortunately for me, I had planned ahead and negotiated extended payment terms with my own vendors. I had 45 to 60 days in which to pay some of my vendors, while I had given my own customers only 30 days in which to pay me. (I paid some of my vendors COD in exchange for payment discounts, but if the vendor did not agree to discounts for early payment, I took the extended terms, using my money for a longer time.)

Well, as the numbers on my accounts receivable grew, the calendar continued to flip also. As soon as an invoice became delinquent, I took steps to recover my money. (You'll be amazed how personal this will become to you!) But, as I mentioned, this is a sticky and uncomfortable position to be in as a business owner. You've delivered the goods and you need to be paid, but you also want to keep the customer.

The first step in collecting your money should be a friendly reminder letter to the customer. In your letter, note that you realize their nonpayment must be an oversight, and you are notifying them of their past-due status because you know they want to keep a good credit history with you. State that you are looking forward to receiving their payment and you appreciate their continued business. Include a copy of the unpaid invoice(s) with your letter. (This will give them everything they need to get moving and get a check out to you.)

If another week goes by and payment is still not received, a phone call is necessary. Call the customer and ask if they received your letter. If they say they received it, ask when you can expect a check to clear up the past-due balance, note this date, and thank them for their assistance. If they say they did not receive your letter, get their fax number and fax a copy of the letter and past-due invoice(s) as soon as you hang up the phone. Wait half an hour and call back to confirm they received the faxed information. Kindly ask when your check is coming and note their response. Document all contacts concerning the collection process, noting when the customer said you should expect their payment.

When the expected payment date arrives and your customer's check is not in your mailbox, you may need to get tougher in your collection process. First, call the customer and ask if the payment was mailed. If they say it was indeed mailed, wait another day or two. You don't want to overreact yet because the customer may be dealing in good faith and the check may indeed be on its way.

If, however, after a couple more days the check does not show up, firmer action is necessary. You may need to contact the supervisor of the person with whom you've been dealing. Possibly there has been a communication breakdown in your customer's office and your bills are not being submitted to their bookkeeper. Notifying a higher-up may resolve your problem and get you paid, but beware, it may also put an end to your relationship with that company. Consider this avenue carefully before acting! Many times I have had to make a judgment call as to whether to proceed with the next firmer collection step, because I knew it could dampen the relations of the future goodwill of that customer. But I quickly learned that some customers were worth having and some were not worth the extra effort in the collection process. And, in my case anyway, large sums were at stake, and I couldn't afford to be wary of the bad feelings my collection efforts could cause! I had a business to run and people to pay!

As a business owner, you will have to make the decision whether to take harsher steps to get paid. You may need to file a lien for unpaid monies (if this is applicable in your case). Many times, when a customer finds there is a lien attached to their property, payment is made quickly. Having a lien attached to one's property makes it difficult to sell or even refinance the property, and owners want to free the property quickly. (Check into the legalities of doing this, of course! Speak with your own attorney for specific information, although you may not choose to use the services of an attorney to file a lien.)

You may need to file suit and attempt to collect your money through the courts. Sometimes, a defendant (your customer) may choose not to even show up in court, whereby your company will win the suit by default. If you have your customer's banking information, take it with you to court, and ask if the judge will garnish the amount due you from your customer's account. (Again, this is a legal issue, so you should seek counsel from an attorney. But I would advise that you look into this area as a final step in collecting your money.)

Over the years, I've found that most people have good intentions, and when given the chance to do the right thing, they will. Again, relationships are important when dealing with collections. If you have a good relationship with your customers and provide good service to them, they will want to keep you as much as you want to keep them!

In pursuing collections, do everything possible to retain your customer without damaging your own business. It is much easier to keep the customer you've got than to replace them!

Managing the Paper Shuffle

The easiest and most efficient way to handle the mountain of paperwork you will begin juggling as a new entrepreneur is to computerize from day one. There are several excellent and user-friendly accounting software packages available today at your local office supply store. Check with your accountant for his recommendation of the one he is most familiar with, as he will most likely be handling your quarterly and annual tax return preparation. Most of the accounting software is so user-friendly that even an accounting novice has no trouble being walked through the initial set-up steps. These programs handle most everything, including invoicing, customer statements, aging reports, check writing, accounts payable reports, sales tax preparation, and federal tax preparation. You will be able to customize the software to your business.

Resources for Help

There are a number of very helpful organizations geared toward helping women in business. Following are some of the organizations you may wish to contact with questions about starting or managing a business:

- Association of Women's Business Centers (AWBC). This is a not-for-profit organization that supports women's entrepreneurship as an avenue to economic self-sufficiency. The AWBC offers mentoring, education, training, business development, and financing opportunities to women.

- American Business Women's Association (ABWA). A networking and support group made up of businesswomen of various occupations. Helps women grow through leadership, education, networking, and national recognition.

- Business Women's Network (BWN). Assists women in starting a business and managing work-life effectiveness.

- National Association of Women Business Owners (NAWBO). Provides networking opportunities for women in business. Has been a women's business association for twenty-five years.

- The International Alliance for Women (TIAW). Unites, supports, and promotes professional women and their networks to work together, sharing resources and leveraging ideas. Offers programs designed to promote economic growth.

- National Women Business Owners Corporation (NWBOC). A national not-for-profit corporation established to increase competition for corporate and government contracts for women business owners. Also provides a national certification program for women-owned businesses.

- SBA's Women's Business Center. Great resource for entrepreneurial women. Can be accessed online.

- Women's Business Centers (WBC). Supported by the U.S. Small Business Administration. Offers training or assistance in finance, management, and marketing matters.

Selling Your Business

When the time comes to sell your business, for whatever reason, there are steps to take to ensure you get the full value of the business you have built. In order to receive the maximum value for your business, plan ahead for its sale. Have an exit strategy!

The Center for Women's Business Research found that 85 percent of both men and women rank price as the most important factor in their decision to sell their business. Not surprisingly, women are more interested than men with the buyer's future plans for the business. Over three quarters of women plan to retire after selling their business, while 22 percent plan to start yet another business!

Like anything else, a business is only worth the amount that someone is willing to pay for it. Potential buyers will likely request copies of tax returns, earnings statements, profit-and-loss reports, budgeted revenues reports, balance sheets, forecasted cash flow reports, and more. Wanting your business to appear as profitable (and attractive) as possible to a buyer is an added incentive to reduce your expenses, increase sales, and run your business as efficiently as possible for a fairly lengthy period of time. Remember: Your asking price must be supported by your financial documentation!

Potential buyers will also want detailed information about all areas of your business including personnel training, shipping and receiving, vehicle maintenance, billing and collections, and more. The most orderly way in which to present this information is through specific systems and procedures manuals for each and every area of your business. Buyers will feel confident that systems are in place for every aspect of your business. They will also have the assurance that they can consult the written procedures after taking over the business.

There are several ways to place a value on a business, and the total value of a business is not based on numbers alone. If your company has developed a loyal customer base and created goodwill based on its service, there is value in this. If you have a specialized marketing method that would be difficult for others to duplicate, there is value in this. If your business is being sold with the property and office building in which it is located, there is, obviously, tremendous value in this. In fact, if you own the property yourself, you may wish to sell only the business and allow its new owner to lease the office space from you, generating continuing rental income from the real estate.

Rather than analyzing and strategizing yourself, consult with your accountant and your attorney regarding the sale of your business. Based on your business's previous performance, future forecasts, and the current economic climate, these professionals will be able to assist you in placing a number on your business.

Marketing

You've got your nice office, your business licenses, a business bank account, and your immediate insurance needs handled. And you're probably exhausted already! Well, now is when the real work begins! You have to pay for that office and fill that bank account. In only a few weeks, your rent will be due, and in a few months your next insurance premium will also be due. But not to worry! Remember: You're a mom. You've given birth. You've handled eight things at once on only two hours' sleep. You can certainly handle this!

First, before you begin the actual task of marketing, you need a few simple, standard materials that will identify your business. You need business cards, company letterhead, brochures, and, if your budget allows, promotional items or giveaways. Don't take this step lightly. Your image is at stake! Within seconds of meeting you a potential customer will make assumptions about your credibility and professionalism. The same can be said for the impression your company's print materials will leave on potential customers. Think about this carefully. If you are a party planner, a fun, whimsical business card is appropriate and lets the public know what to expect of your business. If, however, you are opening a crematorium, the idea of fun is out of the question when designing your company's printed materials.

Think of a way to make your business card stand out from the other thirty business cards tossed haphazardly on a customer's desk or stashed in a drawer. Maybe a photograph on your card is key, so people will put a name with a face, for quick recognition. Possibly a business card that is already precut to be inserted into a Rolodex file, thereby almost ensuring it won't get tossed. Or better yet, use magnetic business cards that your customers put on their refrigerator or filing cabinet as a quick reminder to call you. Consider an unusual color or typeface, although nothing trendy or gaudy. Maybe you could use the back side of your cards to offer a discount off the customer's first purchase or a referral incentive for people if they send business your way. Try to think of something to make people keep and use your cards! Think of your business card as a tool, something to be used by your customers.

Pick a single image or graphic and stick to it. Repetition is key when marketing, especially for a new business. Customers need to see your company's name and logo again and again, in order to commit them to memory.

When ordering your business cards, stationery, and brochures, the higher the quantity ordered, the lower the price will be per unit. So, make sure you choose carefully when designing your logo because you will be paying for thousands of permanent copies of it.

Brochures need not be expensive, but they should be professionally done. Again, your image is at stake. When designing your brochure, clearly and prominently display your company name, phone number, fax number, and business address. Even if your customers may never come to your location, they'll like knowing there is a physical office they can go to if they should ever need to find you. People have faith in what they can see and feel, especially in the case of a new business. Plus, having an office shows a certain degree of dependability and expectations on your part that you will be around next year!

On your brochures, as well as your business cards, clearly and prominently display your name and title, such as Ellen Douglas, President; or Ellen Douglas, Owner & President.

During my years in business, I have encountered many people, both men and women, who apparently are not ready for the evolution of today's female entrepreneur. Now, I do acknowledge that a woman in high heels with a tape measure on a construction site is an oddity, but anyone who knows me also knows I enjoy being a woman and dressing like one. Well, I can't even count the times people have asked, "Oh, do you do the measuring and your husband installs the flooring?" or "Is that the best you can do on the price? Why don't you go back to the office and talk with your husband and see what he can do for me?" or "You must find it difficult working in a man's line of work." Arrghh! Sometimes I'm not sure whether to laugh or cry when responding to these Neanderthals! But I always take the time to politely explain that my husband has never worked with me and that it's actually my own business. With women-owned businesses accounting for 25 to 33 percent of the total business population in the United States, (according to the NFWBO), one should certainly expect to meet a few females who own their own business today!

Frankly, I never cared if my title was President or Janitor, as long as I made money. But, after my initial order of business cards (which listed me as President) ran out, I changed my title to Owner & President. This little change didn't make things perfect, but it has helped. So, depending on the type of industry your business serves, give some thought to your title too!

When designing your business cards and brochures, consider listing your cellular phone number along with your office phone number. It may sound like a headache to have your phone ringing during a soccer game or while you're making a mad dash through the grocery store, but if your customers can't reach you, they will call someone who is accessible and who can immediately assist them.

I was once on a ski vacation in Colorado with my family and had taken the day off from skiing to do a little shopping. Well, lucky for me that I had! Because I was walking around the town, I had my cell phone with me and turned on. I got a call from a regular customer in Florida in need of several carpet jobs the following week. (This happened to be a Realtor who used my company solely because she liked the very personalized attention she got when she called me directly, rather than going through my office. And I was always happy to oblige.) Well, not only did we add those carpet jobs to the following week's schedule, but they spun off two huge referrals of very large oceanfront houses too. So, while always being accessible may not be possible for everyone, it does give a little extra personalized service. And in today's marketplace, word spreads quickly about companies who put their customers' needs first.

If you hold special designations, licensing, or certifications in your field, list these in your brochures as well. Seeing this information in print will instill confidence and lend credibility to your new business. Definitely note that you are licensed and insured, and "bonded," if this is applicable. (Contact your insurance agent for information about becoming bonded, if you will be in your customers' homes.)

Next, note why your business is different from your competitors'. Also put in a guarantee of satisfaction, so your potential customers will know they have nothing to lose by trying your services or products and that you stand behind your company.

And, finally, put in a "call to action." This is a stimulating directive that asks for business. For instance, use statements such as "Don't Delay, Call Today!" or "Call now for a FREE estimate!" Leave your potential customers feeling like they should reach for the phone after looking at your brochure.

While the materials are being completed at the print shop, use this time wisely. Now is the time to begin your marketing plan. (Just as you need a business plan, you need a marketing plan. This is not a coincidence. Always remember the saying: "Those who fail to plan, plan to fail!")

Now, if you have a degree from Harvard Business School, you probably know many of the finer points of marketing, and you are light-years ahead of many of us. But, if you do not, you need not be intimidated by the term *marketing*. Simply stated, it means you will do advertising, promotion, and selling. And because you are a consumer, you already have many opinions about what you want and expect from companies with whom you do business and whose products you utilize. You have formed many opinions about companies and their representatives, as well as about the products they vend. You know what you like and what you don't. And again, because you're a mom, you already have the most exhausting, yet gratifying job on the planet, thus marketing will be a breeze for you!

To begin your marketing plan, simply write down your goals for your business. Next, write down how you think you can achieve each goal. Then identify your market or markets, including one "general market," the people you already know and with whom you do business yourself. Different markets may need a different approach in order to educate them about your business.

Next, make lists. (Don't we moms always make lists?!) One list will be titled "Hard Contacts" and the other will be "Soft Contacts." Your Hard Contacts list will comprise the names of people you likely can count on as customers when they hear you are in business. Or it can be people who, with a little more contact from you, can become a customer. Your Soft Contacts list will contain names of people whose business you will need to work harder to win or whom you will need to educate about your new business. On your Hard List note the names of friends, neighbors, your veterinarian, your hairdresser, your mechanic, your daughter's dance teacher. Basically, this list has people you know well or fairly well and also people with whom you currently have regular dealings. Don't take the time to stop and think and analyze each person's name, just brainstorm and jot it down. Even if that specific individual may not use your product or service, their spouse or relative might! The point is to get the word out to everyone you know that you are now open for business! So, include as many people as possible on the list.

Next, work on your Soft Contacts, which will include the names of your friends' in-laws whom you met at a backyard barbecue; the new people who just moved into your neighborhood; the woman to whom you were introduced at a friend's Mary Kay party; people your friends have suggested may be interested in your products and services. In other words, these leads are weaker; you may need to make a reintroduction or remind them you met last month, but you don't want to discount any possible lead. Remember, we are all consumers! And while every person on your list may not need your products and services today, they may know of someone else who does, or they may need you next month. And you will be surprised by the number of people who love to deal with new businesses to help them get started. I actually have many customers who have told me they prefer to deal with woman-owned businesses, for a variety of reasons.

When you think your two lists are complete, put them aside, but keep them within reach. You will go back to them often to add names. When your daughter's Brownie leader calls, you'll find you are having an *a-ha!* moment and begin scratching down her name. When your lawn man shows up, the lightbulb will go on! Or when your son's football coach calls to ask if you can bring snacks to Saturday's game, you'll find yourself grabbing your Soft Contacts list once again! Keep these lists in your car when you're on the go. After a few days, I guarantee you will have two hearty lists from which to work. And you will be astounded that you know so many people who all are potential customers for your new business!

Now that you've got your lists you are ready to vend your products and services. Now is the time to plan your strategy for getting information to your contacts quickly and efficiently. The methods you choose for delivery of your information may vary depending on the type of business you own, the current economic climate in your immediate area, and, of course, your budget.

Prepare a letter to be printed on your new, professionally printed letterhead stationery. This letter will go to each person on your Hard Contacts list, those people you feel are most likely to need your products or services. Explain that your doors are open at your new location and you are looking forward to being of service. Give a detailed explanation about the products and services you will offer to your customers. Invite them to call you or visit your location for more information.

The letters should be individually addressed to each person on your list. *Do not* send blanket form letters that start out "Dear Sir" or "Dear Madam." We all know what we do when those generic letters arrive in our mailbox. No one will take the time to read them. Instead, take the extra time necessary to insert each person's name and address into each letter and personally sign each letter. This will show your attention to detail, plus make the recipient feel that you think they deserve your attention as a new customer.

Get your letters to your Hard Contacts printed, addressed, and mailed before you worry about your Soft List. Your main objective is to strive for the more definite results first, which would be from your Hard List. Always do the things first that will be more likely to make you money the fastest.

You may choose to cold-call area businesses to distribute literature about your product, introduce yourself, and set up one-on-one appointments with each business owner or decision maker to further discuss your products and services. Cold-calling is really a shot in the dark, and you absolutely must be in the right mindset to do it. If you are not on your game one day, don't cold-call. If you don't feel upbeat and have a positive demeanor, it shows. On days like this, cold-calling is a waste of time, and could actually do more damage by leaving a less than favorable impression on people. You must pump yourself up and think positively, not only about your business, but about yourself. Generally, people gravitate toward positive, upbeat personalities. As a saleswoman, you want to be that personality when dealing with potential customers. Talk yourself into knowing that you are already a success! The power of positive thinking will bring incredible results, and can truly change the outcome of your day in all things!

As I was writing this section I was reminded of a funny story. I do practice what I preach, always trying to think positively and pump up my self-image, but I may just have gone a bit too far a few years back. I was having lunch one day with my best friend, Renata, and when the check came, I looked in my purse and found that I had a bunch of one-dollar bills. Laughing, I said to her, "Hey, if I pay with all these singles, the waitress will probably think I'm a stripper!" Renata cracked up and said, "Oh, get real, she'll probably think you're a waitress!" That brought me back to reality. We still have a great laugh over that incident today. But even if, at times, we carry it too far, keeping a positive image of yourself is certainly better than the flip side! Self-confidence is definitely a good thing . . . in moderation!

I always had to ready myself for cold calls. In the early years of my business, I especially had to make a conscious effort to pump myself up in my own mind before walking through the door of a business, not knowing what to expect on the other side! (Now, fifteen years later, I don't even think about it. So don't worry, you will master this area.)

If you choose to cold-call businesses in your area, invite the employees to your official grand opening, when the public will come by your new shop. Stopping by with a verbal invitation is a great reason to drop in and will leave people with a positive and friendly impression of your business. Be sure to leave at least your business card if not literature and promotional items with your company name.

Women-owned businesses currently generate more than $2 trillion in annual sales. As a new female entrepreneur, you'll be positioned to get in on the fastest growing economic trend in the United States! Print advertising may help in that area and is an avenue worth investigating. While print ads are usually costly, you should explore your options in this area. You can get the advertising rate schedules from your local newspapers, smaller community papers, and trade publications. Local welcome-wagon businesses are also eager to talk with new businesses about being included in their packages for new residents in the area. And while there is a fee for this, you may be able to barter with the company putting together the packages or with the printer handling your advertising materials in order to offset the cost.

When considering advertising rates, don't be too deflated if your budget does not allow for a large color-print ad. Ten smaller ads, run continuously, will likely bring better results than one large ad that you can afford to run just once due to the hefty price tag! Exposure and repetition are the keys to educating the public about your new business. People need to see your business name repeatedly in order for them to commit it to memory. (Again, this is an important reason to choose a simplistic name for your business. People are more likely to recall names if the names are simple.)

Another great way to spread the word about your new business is with a press release. You need not be a journalist or even have writing experience to put together your own press release. All you need is "information of interest." Type your press release and send it to local newspapers via fax or e-mail. At the top, type "For Immediate Release." Make the press release informational, clear, and free of errors! Begin by noting your business name, your name, the location, telephone number, and products and/or services your business offers. Note the date of your grand opening to the general public. After completing your press release, check it over a final time before sending it.

Many newspapers devote a portion of their business section to local businesses. Frequently, a press release like yours will be given to the business section editor and, if you're lucky, also to the editor of the local section. The odds are good that you will be contacted by your local newspaper, asking to spotlight your new business. And before you know it, you could have your new business featured in the newspaper and get some free advertising!

Press releases can be generated for various reasons, even after your business has become established. For instance, if your company lands a major contract with the local school board, or you've just completed a renovation at a major hotel, or maybe you've hired a new employee. These are all examples of reasons to send a press release.

After you have completed your first press release and are awaiting word from your local newspaper that they will feature your business, you may feel like it's time for a break. Not yet! The clock is still ticking and you need to generate revenue. You cannot afford to waste even a single day. Use your time effectively and efficiently to market. It's time to once again contact those persons listed on your Hard Contacts list, who have by now received your personal letters about the opening of your business. The chances are pretty good that because you know these people, they are aware of your new location and have hopefully made a mental note to stop by after receiving your recent letter. Before they have time to cool on the idea of dropping by, it is a good idea to invite them to a private grand opening at your new location. Depending on your type of business, your invitation could be for a specific day, when you will open your doors for the entire day, and people can drop by at their leisure, much like an open house. Or, it could be an evening affair, with set starting and ending times.

When planning your private grand opening, visit your local print shop once again to have simple, tasteful invitations printed using your business name and logo on the front. Inside, ask your guests for "the pleasure of their company" as you celebrate the opening of your new business. (A tip for saving on your printing expense: Allow the printer to print his business name on the back of each invitation along the bottom edge, in return for a discount on your order.)

No matter what your type of business, on the day of the private grand opening celebration, you should be prepared to display your wares and answer questions. Show off all your products and be prepared to take orders at that time. If you are a one-woman office, enlist the help of a friend or two to assist you during your grand opening. A few extra pairs of hands filling glasses and greeting guests will allow you the time to visit with all of your guests.

Provide easy-to-eat finger foods and dainty desserts, along with several types of cold beverages and hot coffee. The decision to serve wine or other alcohol in your place of business is a personal one. Be advised that you may be prohibited from serving alcohol on leased premises without a proper permit. And, more important, should a guest be injured or cause injury to another due to the alcohol he consumed at your function, you and your business could be held liable.

In preparation for your private grand opening, thoroughly "spiff up" all offices, showrooms, warehouse areas, and restrooms. Put away any personal information and documents in your offices. Assume that a few of your guests will wander around checking out every nook and cranny of your office during the evening, just like people snooping in the medicine cabinet during a party at home!

Even if you don't take orders from each person in attendance, you will most definitely develop many solid leads and possibly even collect a few referrals. You will quickly learn that business is all about relationships. The relationships you build are critical to the success of your business!

Next, after your private grand opening, schedule your official opening for the public, the date you provided the newspaper in your press release. This is the day when you will officially open your doors to the general public, put out your banners, and announce to all that you are ready to be of service! Provide light refreshments in your showroom or display areas, inviting patrons to linger awhile. Expect to have a few children accompany their parents as they visit your new business. Have small toys and books available for them, and, if possible, a small television with a children's video playing, set off in a part of your showroom where the children are visible to their parents, but still entertained and occupied.

Again, depending on the nature of your business, you can offer free samples of your products as people browse your shop. Provide literature about your business, being as informational as possible. Give your potential customers something to take with them when they leave your shop. Be sure your company name, logo, and phone number are on all items you give away. Keep your name in front of them! Depending on your budget for promotional items, you may choose to provide your potential customers with a computer mouse pad (they'll see it every day); drink coasters (Who throws those away? You can never have too many!); or even pens, which are inexpensive and can be purchased in huge lots.

One thing that I found to be extremely popular and inexpensive was "Things to Do" pads. I had them printed with my company name, logo, and phone number at the top of each page. Below that was the "Things to Do Today" heading, with the numbers one through twelve underneath and a ruled line beside each. (On the first line, print "Call _____ today!" inserting your own company name. Don't forget what these pads are really for!) I actually had many of my commercial customers calling to ask for more pads when their office ran out. It was a great opportunity to get through their door again to drop off more pads. Again, keep your name in front of them and build a relationship with your customers!

During your official opening, have a free drawing for some of your products or services. You could offer a small color television or dinner for two at a local restaurant as the prize for the winner of the drawing. (I know, you are seeing dollar signs and wondering why you are giving away things when you need to be bringing in money at this point, but there is a point to this!) When patrons fill out your preprinted drawing coupons, have them list their name, phone number, address, and which of your products or services they may require in the near future. At the end of your opening, you will have a fishbowl of possible leads! Plus, you will now be able to drop each person a thank-you card for stopping in to check out your new shop, and you can add these people to a mailing list for future use. Keep your name in front of them!

At the end of your opening day, have a legitimate drawing for your prize. Call the winner and invite them to stop by to pick up their item or gift certificate. If nothing else, you will be building goodwill, and the winner of your drawing is sure to tell a few friends about their new television or dinner out on the town, compliments of your business.

You are probably wondering what to do with your Soft Contacts list. Well, by now, you've had your private grand opening with the people on your Hard Contacts list whom you know well; you've put out your press release; hopefully, your local newspaper has spotlighted your business or, better still, run an article on your new venture; you may have met people from other local businesses when you were cold-calling and inviting them to your official opening; and you've had your official opening to the general public. So, it's safe to assume that at least some of those people on your Soft Contacts list have heard about your business at this point. It is now time to get in front of those people.

The letter that you previously prepared and sent to your Hard Contacts can be used again now. Simply insert each person's name and address at the top of each letter. Again, send each person on your Soft Contacts list a letter addressed specifically to that person and signed by you. General, blanket-type correspondence will definitely get tossed with the junk mail!

After about a week has passed, and enough time has elapsed for your recipients to have received your letters, phone each person individually. Identify yourself and your business and state that you are calling to ensure that your letter was received. Ask if you might be of service. If the phone call is successful, you will follow up and meet with your potential customer to close a sale. If the call is not a success, tell the person to keep you in mind for the future and invite them to stop by your shop sometime. Always end the call on a friendly, positive note, mentioning that you've appreciated their time. In today's busy world, you will not be seen as an intrusion if you acknowledge the busy lives of your potential customers.

Keep a log of your follow-up phone calls and the result of each contact made, be it positive or negative. This will serve as a reference of how to deal with each person in the future. If your contact was a success and you were able to close a sale, maybe your customer will need to make another purchase in three months. You will be able to contact your customer at that time and again offer your services. If the contact was not a success, you will be able to look back and see that you noted your potential customer "was on their way out the door" and couldn't talk, so therefore you never got very far on the phone; or perhaps your contact had just bought the item your business offers, but they invited you to phone them again in about six months. A log of your contact results will prove very helpful in handling your next contact. And, people will appreciate the fact that you "remembered" your last conversation with them.

Never just blindly blanket your contacts with mailers or advertising literature. Have a follow-up plan if you send mailings to people and act on it!

The Internet

You may wish to reach customers in a broader, global market. If so, the fastest and most innovative way in which to get your product or service to the masses is via the Internet. Today's technology offers so many options to entrepreneurs!

Use the three big search engines, Yahoo!, Google, and MSN, to submit your business information to every free directory possible. This information will be collected and put into a listing, detailing information about your business.

Today people choose to log onto the Internet for just about everything: news, economic indexes, solutions to daily problems, recipes for dinner, consumer feedback, shopping, and finding businesses in their area. Having your business listed on an Internet search engine is great, because customers will be driven to your business, ready for you to fill their needs.

In setting up your listing, you will need to come up with twenty-five to thirty specific keywords that, when typed in as search terms, will steer Internet users to your listing. When using search engine advertising, you will want to track what is working. To assist in this, you will receive reports of how many people visited and with which "keywords" they were steered to your listing. This will enable you to fine-tune your keywords after you see what is working. Again, use the reports and data to steer your marketing efforts.

When you are ready to take your Internet marketing to the next level, you may wish to look into a Website for your business. There are companies you can hire to set up your site, from start to finish. Fees and services will vary, so check around and compare. There are also online site-building tools that will assist you in setting up your own site.

No matter which method you select for creating your Website, be proactive in the site's implementation. After the site is up and working, track your traffic to ensure you're getting all you can from your Website.

Handling the First Sales

Great! So the marketing efforts have paid off and you've gotten a few sales! Now what? Well, first, make sure you handle your initial customers with kid gloves. Go the extra mile to provide the best service imaginable. Go overboard! If you're providing a service, do something extra at no charge so that you'll make a great impression and your customer will remember you. If you're providing a product, toss in a little something extra when transacting the sale. Invite them to visit your shop again or to call for your service again. Building a strong customer base is critical, especially for new businesses.

Immediately send a Thank You card to your customer, thanking them for their business. Tell them you look forward to being of service again.

When it comes to customer relations, just think of how *you've* felt when you were the customer. Don't you always remember the businesses that provide great service, making you feel valuable to them? Don't you appreciate when a company does a little something extra or throws in a freebie from time to time? Isn't it a good feeling to visit a store and have the help remember you and treat you like a friend? And don't you *talk* about these businesses to your friends and family? Which leads me to the next step: REFERRALS.

REFERRALS

After you've serviced your new customer or sold them your products, don't stop there! *Ask* for referrals from your satisfied customers. People are happy to refer their friends and family to companies that have provided them with superior service.

Turn one sale into several, simply through the referrals of a single, satisfied customer.

You can ask for referrals through a personal note, an e-mail, or a mailer about your "Referral Program," through which you will gratefully provide a free product or service in exchange for each referral sent to you.

Referrals are powerful, because they come from customers you've already dealt with and to whom you've provided exceptional service. What better advertising is there than a satisfied customer?

But make sure you thank the people who send you additional business! Your Thank You can be in the form of a card, a voucher for a free service, a free product, a gift certificate, or anything else you think your initial customer might appreciate. Simply saying "Thank You" and expressing your gratitude will cement your relationship with your customers and ensure their future business. *Remember:* You don't want a one-time customer. You want to build ongoing relationships with your customers!

The Choices and the Children

Recently, while I was in Panama, it struck me how family-oriented the Panamanians seemed to be. I saw many examples of Panamanians putting their families first. A cab driver in Panama City explained that we were his last fare of the evening, as every Friday night he and his wife take their boys, ages four and eight, to Kentucky Fried Chicken for dinner, and he couldn't be late. A woman in Bocas Del Toro ran a breakfast and lunch café so she could be available for her children after school. In Boquete, two brothers worked together daily running a whitewater rafting company that serviced the tourists. And in several of the local restaurants in Boquete, we met families who worked side by side running the business and serving the customers.

Making Choices

In the United States, I think, most families try to do the same: keeping families together while providing for them. And while all households may not fit everyone's definition of "conventional," it seems like each family figures out what works best for them. Statistics quoted in the March 2007 issue of *Empowering Women* showed that in 55 percent of U.S. households, women bring in more than half of the household's total income. While this information may not be surprising, it definitely shows that women are not afraid to take the leap for the betterment of their families. And I think it also shows that today's dads are supportive of women's evolving roles in society.

But still, many women struggle with the question of what is best for their family. Should they get a job? Should they start their own business? Should they be a stay-at-home mom? Is there a way to have it all?

Well, if you're a mom questioning your next move, simply make a list of the pros and cons for each scenario with which you're struggling. This will help to clarify things for you. When you can see it all in black and white, you'll be able to organize your thoughts and finally make a decision, one way or another.

I have friends who tell me there is no way in the world they'd deal with the stress or time constraints my business puts on me. I also have friends who, like me, specifically chose to become entrepreneurial moms solely for the flexibility and financial rewards it provides their families. Then, of course, there are those friends who prefer the sane, structured schedule of a nine-to-five job, with its predictability that enables them to "switch off" at the end of the day and be Mom again by dinnertime. I respect all of these choices. I think all women should do whatever feels right for them and that we should all be thankful to have so many choices available to us.

Children Learn What They Live

We've all heard it said that "children learn what they live." Of course, there has always been the question of "nature versus nurture" when it comes to raising children. But I am a strong believer in the "nurture" side of the argument. As such, I feel that if, as a mother, I can show my children the endless possibilities available to them, that they will want to reach for them.

Because I believe that a child's environment is so very important, I try to live a life that my children can look up to. And, while I am far from perfect as a mother or an entrepreneur, I am always on the lookout for those "teaching moments": situations and incidents that I can use as teaching tools with my children. As a mom, I can tell you that it is very gratifying when I see that a lesson or two has actually sunk in with my children!

For example, for a time I was dealing with a situation at my office where finances were tight due to a few delinquent customers who carried large balances with my business. My daughter was at my office one day during this period and overheard my phone conversation with the controller for one of the late-paying companies. After I hung up the phone, I explained to her why I was stressed and I also explained to her that I had to budget my business funds carefully for a while as I pursued the collection of the money owed to me. (As I said earlier, my children have seen the good and the bad sides of my entrepreneurial role; I want them to know the realities of life.)

Well, some time later, my daughter went on a school trip to Washington, D.C., with her classmates. (As a young teenager, she had begged me not to tag along as a chaperone, and I reluctantly and painfully agreed to let her spread her wings.) To my surprise, when she returned from her trip, she still had nearly all the spending money we'd loaded onto her Visa BUXX card. (I know that at age thirteen I would have spent it all!) When I asked her why she didn't spend more, she said she wanted to be able to use the money for something she really wanted when she got home, so she was careful to budget her money. It did my heart good to realize that she was learning to budget her funds, something she'll do for years to come, even into adulthood.

In our home, we provide our children an allowance, solely for the purpose of teaching them how to manage money. The allowance isn't tied to chores, because as a member of the family, they're expected to pitch in around the house anyway. When they receive their weekly allowance, they put in into their own plastic bank with three separate sections. One section is marked "SPENDING," one is "SAVE FOR BIG TICKET ITEMS," and one is "INVEST." The kids have pooled their big ticket savings for items like a surfboard or roller blades. The investment money is used to purchase shares of stock in the kids' names from time to time. And the spending money gives them pocket money. Well, recently I was so proud to find that, unbeknownst to me, my young son had been taking large amounts of his own spending money to school each week to contribute to a fund used to provide for a Haitian girl and her family. When I told him I was proud of his generosity, he said, "Well, Mom, last week I gave ten dollars, so the family can buy a goat!" He was quietly helping someone else and feeling good about himself while doing it. My little guy was learning to "give back."

One day, several years ago, I had my son at my office. I think he was about six at the time. One of my flooring installers came to me with a problem be had encountered on a job. (Truth be told, he took a shortcut in the installation process and had created the problem himself.) He wanted me to work things out for him and deal with the homeowner on his behalf. I explained that if he was to continue subcontracting jobs through me in the future, he was going to have to repair his mistake and smooth things over with the customer. When he left, my son asked me why I wouldn't do what the installer had asked. I explained that if I had, then there would be no lesson in it and the installer would put us in the same situation again, unless he knew I'd hold him accountable.

Not long after this brief incident, my son was playing outside one Saturday afternoon and took a break to come inside for lunch. While eating, he told me that the neighborhood kids were taking sides and not playing together, like all kids do. My "mom instinct" was to march outside and handle things, but my son said that if I did that then no one would learn how to get along on their own. Well, he was right. As soon as he finished his lunch, he went back outside to play peacemaker, and before long I saw that all of the kids were playing together again. I was pleased to see my son had worked out the problem himself and was learning about conflict resolution!

Because we want our children to be independent, my husband and I have always used every opportunity to let them do things for themselves and learn. (I have to admit that, as a mom, sometimes this is hard for me, since I instinctively want to handle everything myself!) Since I obviously end up running some work-related errands with my kids at times, I let them participate when possible. The kids are happy to retrieve the company mail, add up the bank deposits, deal with the tellers in the bank, and help navigate our travels by reading the road signs. Because my daughter is thirteen, she also sometimes helps me with filing, both at work and at home. I find that the kids enjoy learning and being a part of things.

We let the children speak up for themselves in all circumstances from dealing with salespeople in a department store to buying movie theater tickets, to dealing with the baggage handlers at the airport. These simple tasks have enabled the kids to carry themselves comfortably, confident in their own abilities. As a result, my eleven-year old son can walk into a crowded room, introduce himself and offer handshakes, all without hesitation. And he can debate issues about which he's passionate even better than most adults I know. My thirteen-year old daughter is totally at ease with herself, comfortable holding conversations with adults and handling most any situation with which she is faced.

I think that because children learn what they live, ours have watched as we've grown our businesses, traveled, been in social situations, made financial decisions, and dealt with all types of people. And it's because of these things that they are well-rounded, independent individuals, ready to take on the world. (Check with me in a few years—I'm keeping my fingers crossed!)

Learn to Be Selfish!

If you are an entrepreneurial mom or are considering becoming one, chances are that you're a take-control, in-charge woman. I fit that description too, and at times I've wished I could let go a little bit!

Take it from me, when your business reaches the point where you can take some time away from it, take it! And take it completely!

Years ago I would schedule time off for family vacations, but I always took my cell phone with me and checked in with the office each and every day that I was away. Looking back, I can't believe I didn't realize how crazy it was. I was obsessed! I constantly had to know what was going on and whether there were any traumas that I needed to know about. I never really relaxed and "turned off"!

My husband thought I was nuts, as I obsessively searched for pay phones throughout London. And then, I was really agitated when I couldn't get a phone line to the United States from our hotel room in Paris. (The next day, however, I fed my control obsession by standing in the rain and calling my office from a pay phone while my family enjoyed their lunch inside a nice restaurant.) Once, I was so concerned over a customer's order that I called the office to check on its progress—from the side of a mountain in Aspen, Colorado. I was really unnerved when my cell phone wouldn't get a signal as we RV'd through Alaska. And I remember the feeling of relief when we were in the mountains of Virginia and I found a corner of the property where I could get a weak cell phone signal if I held my head at the just the right angle while I talked!

Then, one day, when my children were still young, I realized that my overcontrolling ways were causing me much more stress than the benefits I was getting from my business. Fortunately, I was finally able to learn to rely on others, and trust they'd handle things in my absence. But to be honest, it took a lot of work to get to that point.

I'm so thankful that I finally realized that the business will always be there, but the precious family time won't. The only reason I'm even mentioning this is so that other women will not waste the time and

I honestly think that without our children, our lives would be really boring. Take for instance, the simple act of ordering a pizza for delivery. Pretty basic, right? My husband had called in our pizza order one night, and when it hadn't arrived an hour later he was getting a bit irritated. Things didn't get better when the pizza guy finally showed up. He rang the doorbell near the pool patio first. But just as my husband went to open that door, he had moved around to the front door and was ringing that bell. (In all fairness, it is difficult to know which door to come to at our house if it's your first time there, especially after dark.) Unaware that our toddler was listening, Jerry mumbled, under his breath, "What a dumb---!" as he walked around to the front door. As he was paying for the pizza, Jerry felt our son hanging on his leg. Jared pointed to the delivery guy and said, "Daddy, here's the dumb---!" What does this little anecdote have to do with being an entrepreneurial mom? Well, a week later I found out that my company was tiling the delivery guy's floor!

energy I did in the early years of my business. Feeling like you have to always be in control is exhausting!

Now, if I'm going away, I leave someone in charge or even close the office for a few days. Closing the office while I'm away takes some planning, of course, but with some forethought and clever scheduling, I've found it sometimes is the best answer. For instance, my office manager is also a mother of young children. If I'm planning to take a week off with my kids for spring break, I'll usually give her the week off too. Or, sometimes I'll close the week of Christmas, which is typically a slower time, and this gives everyone a little more time to get ready for the holiday. I just plan ahead, and the business doesn't miss a beat now!

So, if you're already in business, give yourself permission to take time off! (I have no doubt that as an entrepreneurial mom you've more than earned it!) If you're just starting your business, learn to be selfish and really take time off with your family to recharge your batteries. Now that I've learned to do that, I can fully enjoy our family time and I return to my business mentally and physically refreshed.

Maximize Family Time

While all entrepreneurial moms want to put their families first, the unsettling reality is that business sometimes creeps in to interrupt our daily routines. If you have a business that ends at a specific time each and every day, then you are extremely fortunate. But for many entrepreneurial moms, over the course of a workweek, their cell phone rings during baseball games, while grocery shopping, and at dinnertime. And it is rarely a welcome sound—to them or to their family!

Depending on the nature of your business, you may be able to turn off your phone every day at 5:00 and simply return your messages the next morning. I, however, was not so fortunate when I first started my business. If I had an especially busy day, it was necessary for me to place my customers' orders in the evening. I frequently had to call the next day's customers to verify their appointment times (most people work during the day, and if I was to make personal contact, I had to call in the evening). And I would almost always have to talk with my sub-contractors at the end of the day to ensure they'd completed my customers' installations. I must say, I really hated the intrusions during the evening. But I should have anticipated what it would be like, because even when I was at the hospital having my labor induced for the birth of my daughter, I was on the phone, still trying to take care of everything!

Fortunately, however, things did get easier later on, when I was able to hire some office help! Then, I just had to back off and let them do their jobs—a process that took some getting used to, as I said, since I'd been doing everything myself for a while!

After a few hectic years of trying to balance work and family, I finally figured out that although there were some things I *couldn't* control, I would simply have to control those things that I *could*. This revelation came after the birth of my second child, when my daughter was two years old. I still remember holding my new baby son and thinking that it only seemed like last week that I was holding my firstborn!

Realizing that time stops for no one, I sought ways to maximize family time whenever possible, even building in certain activities to my regular schedule so that I didn't get too busy to fit them in! I also started taking off one day during the workweek to spend more time with my children. This took some maneuvering and scheduling, as my business was still operating during these times. But it was worth it. And I usually kept my sitter on this day, so that I could take my daughter out in the morning alone and then, while she napped later, I could have uninterrupted time with the baby in the afternoon. My business was still less than three years old, so I had to be available via telephone for customers, installers, deliveries, and so on, and the arrangement wasn't perfect, but what is? When you're a mom, as we all know, sometimes it's just a matter of making it work.

If you're an entrepreneurial mom already or you're thinking about giving it a try, you'll need to face the reality early on that you are only human and can only keep so many plates spinning at once! Once I figured this out for myself, life got so much easier for me. And after I started allowing myself to schedule extra family time, I began to finally feel fulfilled.

So, don't assume that if you own a business you cannot schedule time with your family too. By family time, I don't mean time spent in the car driving the carpool to school, or time together while the kids do homework and you prepare dinner, or time on Sunday while the kids eat breakfast and you read the newspaper. Believe me, your kids won't remember these times. They will, however, remember the times that you arranged your schedule to be with them, undistracted and completely in-tune with them. They'll remember that you took the time to talk with them about their opinions and their dreams, or the times you just let loose and got silly with them.

I believe children want the reassurance that they're valued and that their parents make time just for them. No matter how busy you get with your business, make a point to connect with your children. Sometimes scheduling family activities is great and other times just spending one-on-one time with each child can be so rewarding. I find that my children open up more when we're alone, when they're not competing with their sibling for time or attention.

While writing this book, I asked my daughter, now thirteen, to be honest with me about how it's been for her having an entrepreneurial mom. (I was holding my breath waiting for her answer, as you might imagine.) Kaitlyn said, "Well, when I was little, I wanted you home more, but as I got older, I realized that it was better that you owned your business so you could make your own hours." She went on to say, "Even though Miss Dorothy (the sitter) was like a grandmother to me, she wasn't a substitute for you or Dad reading me a book." As we talked, she said she felt there were positive and negative things about having an entrepreneurial mom. When I asked what she's observed over the years, she thought for a minute then said, "You have to be firm with people to get the job done and for them to respect you!" Then she added, "At least when I start my vet practice after college, I know I can always come to you and Dad with questions, so I guess it's been a good thing!"

Relieved that I had gotten one child's stamp of approval, I moved on to my son, now eleven. Jared's response was, "I'm glad you always had time to come to all my games, awards, and stuff at school." I kept press-ing him for more, but intent on getting outside to play basketball, he just replied, "Gee, Mom! I wouldn't know what it's like to have a mom who's *not* an entrepreneur!"

What Is Success, Anyway?

On June 10, 2005, I awoke, opening my eyes to the reality that I was forty years old. I lay in bed, unmoving, not sure if I wanted to acknowledge the day. As I had done on my thirtieth birthday, I began to reflect on my life. While I had an awesome husband and the two most incredible children on the face of the earth (don't we all?), I was disappointed that in my forty years I had not made a huge social contribution to the world by doing something major like curing cancer, erasing famine, or ridding the planet of AIDS. I thought, How does one live half a lifetime without effecting change? Realizing I had a busy day ahead, I decided to drag myself from my bed and accept the fact that after forty years, the world was unchanged by my presence.

I went through my day, running errands and keeping appointments, as usual. I knew my husband and kids had plans to take me to dinner to celebrate the "Big Four-O" so I bought a new outfit, trying to cheer myself up a bit. (Retail therapy usually does it for me.)

At 7:15 that evening, my husband pulled our car into the parking lot of a beachfront hotel, which I found extremely odd. I looked at my son and daughter in the backseat, who were exchanging nervous glances. As we entered the hotel, we were met by a woman who, suspiciously enough, seemed to know my husband. She led us, not to a table at the hotel's restaurant, but to a set of double doors, which she threw open. A unison scream of "Surprise!" hit me as I was nearly knocked over physically. I couldn't even take it all in as I was greeted with hugs from friends and family who had traveled from all over the country to be with me on my special night. I lost track of my husband and my children in the crowd of familiar faces, as someone handed me a drink and the band started playing. Believe me, anyone who knows me well knows I am never speechless and I hate to be unprepared. I was so overwhelmed as I hugged everyone and cried as I greeted some of the most special people in my life, so many of whom I had not been face-to-face with in ages!

The evening flew by at lightning speed as we ate dinner, danced, and caught up with one another. The atmosphere was electrified and the room aglow with all the warmth contained within its walls that night. And the party atmosphere only intensified as my friends and family delighted in exchanging "Mary" stories at the microphone as I turned several shades of crimson.

A very good friend of ours, Steve, a professional videographer, even put together a video of my life, complete with photos and music, which was shown during the evening. This provided both laughs and tears for many of us and will always be a treasured keepsake for me. Thankfully, Steve even created a video of my party that night as well, so I can relive my special evening whenever I want!

Finally, when the evening was winding to a close, I took the opportunity to take the microphone and express my heartfelt thanks to everyone. With a lump in my throat, I explained how I had awakened that morning feeling a bit disappointed that after forty years I hadn't achieved some huge, earth-shattering, universe-changing success with which to leave the world one day. But that now, as I looked around the room at the faces of those I loved, I realized that my world was far richer and fuller than I could have ever imagined. Smiling back at me were the faces of all the people whose presence in my life had made me who I was after forty years! And what a birthday gift it was to be in their presence! I realized that night I was a very blessed woman, whose riches far exceeded any material wealth I could have accumulated.

My husband and my children thought they had given me a big party, but what they really gave me that night was a new perspective and a fuller heart. After forty years, I finally knew what success really was, and it was all around me that night. And, I must admit, I have kept my "Birthday Girl" crown. It sits atop my closet shelf as a happy reminder of a terrific, life-changing evening.

Nearly eighteen months since my Big Four-O, I've had many opportunities to think about all the people who took the time to travel to Florida for one special evening with me. There were people there who had known me since my birth and many special new friends too. All of these people knew little snippets of my past. But as I began writing this book, focusing on women, primarily on mothers, I really began thinking about all the different women who had come together that night with me. What a strong group of women I have in my circle! There was a woman who had grown up in a poor coal-mining town in West Virginia, yet gone on to raise five children and become educated, well-read, and well-traveled. There was a beautiful young woman who currently battles multiple sclerosis while parenting a toddler and holding down a professional position that requires her to travel frequently. There was a woman who single-handedly had raised two incredibly bright daughters and was running a catering business to help put them through two top universities. And before that, she ran a cleaning business so she could work while her girls were in school and still be available to them each day when they arrived home. There was a woman who had bravely survived the suicide of her teenage son and somehow still held her family together in the wake of the tragedy. There were cancer survivors, victims of child abuse, children of alcoholics, diabetics, women who had lost their children, women who had suffered multiple miscarriages, women dealing with mental illness in their family, women who had lost their spouses. Although I knew all these women and their stories, many of them had not met one another until the night of my party, and still do not know one another's history. When I look back on that night and think of the women in that room, I am in awe of the strength they all possess. Nearly all of them have overcome hardship and persevered to become productive and successful women, many of whom are entrepreneurial moms, just like me.

WHAT IS SUCCESS, ANYWAY?

And so, as you close this book, take with you the strength of all the women in your own circle as you move ahead in your own life, cutting a path for yourself as an entrepreneurial mom!

101 Time Savers, Stress Reducers, and Inspirations for Moms

When I first began to compile this list, it was my initial intention to gear it specifically to entrepreneurial moms. I soon realized, however, that *all* moms share some of the same obstacles, whether they're stay-at-home moms, working moms, or entrepreneurial moms. I also realized that all moms can benefit from this type of information. I hope you'll take from this list some time savers that will make your life easier or some inspiration to make your heart lighter!

1. Pack your children's lunches the night before each school day. If you take your lunch to the office, prepare yours as well. The next morning, you'll be glad to find one less task to handle!

2. Have your children select their clothes the night before school. You can check their selection and make adjustments if needed, but this allows them some freedom of choice, plus it teaches responsibility.

3. Put away homework and books in backpacks and book bags the night before. Have your children get in the habit of putting any papers requiring parents' signatures or attention in one specific location, such as a file tray beside where they store their book bags. This will allow you to check the file, review the materials, and return them to your child if necessary. Consider this your "in-basket" at home, and this, too, will soon become routine for both you and your children.

4. Teach your children to sort laundry by lights, darks, and towels. Keep three clothes hampers in the laundry room, each marked with

its contents. If your children are very young, you can simply put pictures of the type of items each hamper contains. This will save time as you will no longer have to sort the laundry before putting it in the washer. And, if you're in a mad dash out the door, you can stop to put in a quick load, again without taking time to sort.

5. Keep one clothes basket per child in your laundry room. As you fold clothes, put them in their respective baskets. Once a week, have the children put away their own laundry.

6. Put a shoe rack in your laundry room or a convenient place near the back door like a mud room. As each family member comes home, they can remove their shoes, placing them on the rack. This will save wear and tear on your carpet, plus allow for longer periods between vacuuming.

7. If you have preschool-age children, teach them to put away their own clothes and dress themselves by putting pictures on their drawers of what's inside! Put a picture of a shirt on their shirt drawer and a picture of pajamas on their pajama drawer, and so on. The kids will feel a sense of accomplishment and learn responsibility at the same time.

8. Purchase and install an "instant-hot" faucet beside your regular kitchen sink faucet. This unit provides near-boiling water for instant coffee, soup, or mac and cheese, saving you time. Cost: Only about $80.

9. Keep a basket beside the door you from which you exit each day. Keep your car keys in this basket, so you'll have to make this your final stop on the way out the door each day. Put the oft-forgotten things, such as shopping lists, bills to mail, dry-cleaning stubs, library books to return, theater tickets, prescriptions to refill, etc., in this basket. This is a great time-saver for the entrepreneurial mom as she makes her way through her day, blending business and personal errands as time allows.

10. Purchase a garment steamer. The $75 to $100 cost is minimal, compared to the time saved over ironing. (And the additional uses for this appliance are endless. The steamer also can be used to remove "furniture dents" from carpet after re-arranging furnishings; steam stains out of carpets; remove water stains from shower doors; remove wallpaper; and who knows what else!)

11. If you wear contacts or eyeglasses, keep a spare pair at your office in case of emergency.

12. Start a carpool with other parents in the neighborhood. This takes some planning, but it works great for getting kids to and from school, sporting events, club activities, and especially those endless weekend activities that leave all parents "pulled in opposite directions." Again, use your day planner to keep track of this.

13. Every time you get out of your car when you return home each day, take out three things to be put away or thrown away to keep your car free of clutter.

14. Kids have a function at school coming up? Don't offer to bake! It's okay to be the mom who brings the sodas or paper products! Keep a surplus of these items in your pantry so you don't have to make a special trip to the supermarket.

15. Create a chore chart for older children. Use a dry-erase board and change each child's assignments daily, depending on what household chore needs to be done; or create a more permanent chart with specific items that each child is responsible for each day of the week. A few age-appropriate chores are a good lesson in responsibility for all children. Plus, it shows the children how to work as part of a team to make the household function.

16. Never let junk mail hit your desk or your kitchen counter! As soon as you retrieve it from your mailbox, if you know you won't use it, toss it out!

17. Every morning when you open your eyes, be thankful that you did!

18. Take the time to talk to each of your children and tell them why you think they're special.

19. The next time you're at your local discount store, buy a couple of extra gifts for use at your children's friends' birthday parties. Games, paints, and crafts are usually a safe bet for either gender in the younger crowd. Gift certificates to local stores or movie theaters are great to keep on hand as gifts for older kids.

20. Keep on hand several items that would suffice as teacher-appreciation gifts, hostess gifts, or thank-you gifts. Some suggestions: scented candles, potpourri, picture frames, holiday ornaments, stationery, movie theater tickets.

21. Collect all your gift wrap, tissue paper, ribbon, and gift cards in one place and store them with tape, scissors, and a pen. You won't have to spend time digging through drawers and closets when it's time to wrap gifts!

22. Wear your seat belt. Your children need you!

23. Buy a fabric nail apron from your local home improvement store. Have your child store any loose crayons, markers, or colored pencils in the pockets. He can wear it while working at his easel, then tie it to the back of his chair when not in use.

24. Keep a bowl of fresh fruit on hand. It makes a quick healthy snack for everyone in the family and is easy to grab on the run.

25. Decrease your laundry loads by having each family member use their towel after bathing, then hang it up for another use before throwing it into the laundry. After all, they're clean when they towel off!

26. Put the vitamins beside the coffeemaker. Each morning take a vitamin as you get your first cup of coffee. Getting your vitamins is a great stress-reducer.

27. Keep a nap mat, child-sized blanket, and travel pillow in your office for your child. As an entrepreneurial mom, there will be times when you have your child at your office, and if it's naptime, you'll be thankful your little guy can get in his scheduled break.

28. Give blood. Take twenty minutes to stop by your local blood bank and help someone else. This selfless act will make you feel good and remind you that you're part of something bigger than yourself.

29. Share stories of your own childhood with your children so they'll get to know who you were before you became Mom.

30. Get up thirty minutes before the kids. This will give you time for a shower and a cup of java before the morning's mad dash!

31. Doesn't it seem that kids outgrow their shoes about every two weeks? As an entrepreneurial mom, you're on the go, and chances are you're on the road too. To save time shopping for your children's shoes, make an outline of their foot. Keep this with you, and when you have a few minutes between clients, drop into the shoe store, match it up with a shoe that is just a bit bigger than your outline, and you'll be on your way in a matter of minutes. (Of course, we all realize this only works until they're about eleven, at which time we mothers completely lose all sense of style and have no business trying to pick out their shoes. So, enjoy this tip while you can.)

32. Can't find your lint brush or lint roller? No problem. Just slip a pair of pantyhose over your hand. It works!

33. Time to mail out Christmas cards already? Save time by having the kids put stamps and return-address labels on the envelopes.

34. Leave duplicate cleaning supplies in each bathroom of your home. This saves time normally spent collecting and putting away supplies. Plus, you can quickly scrub your shower before you bathe if the supplies are nearby.

35. Keep plastic bags from your grocery store on hand in a cabinet or pantry. They have a million uses and are especially handy when your kids have a sleepover and a dozen kids get out of the pool and each needs a place to store a wet bathing suit after they change.

36. Leave lavender potpourri or aromatic warmers in your bedroom and bath. Lavender is known for its relaxing, stress-reducing qualities.

37. Need an invigorating pick-me-up? Use granulated sugar as a shower scrub, then follow with peppermint- or citrus-scented lotion.

38. Keep hairspray in your office—not just for your hair, but also to remove ink from a white blouse.

39. Hairspray or rubbing alcohol also removes ink from a car's headliner after your toddler finds a spare pen in the backseat.

40. Keep thank-you cards on hand at home and in the office. You'll be able to grab one and jot a quick note while the gratitude is fresh.

41. Teach your teenage daughter to change a tire. Teach your teenage son to change a diaper. The day will come when they will both thank you!

42. Traveling with the kids? If it's a car trip, calculate the time you'll be in the car. Collect inexpensive treats for each child and place them in small bags labeled with each child's name. Dole out the goodies every hour. The kids love the anticipation, and it keeps them on good behavior.

43. Remove the visitor(s) chairs from in front of your desk at your office. This is a clear sign that you're busy and cannot stop to talk. Replace the chairs for meetings or interviews as needed.

44. Keep a spare car key at your office. While you could call the auto club to unlock your car's door, the hour you'll waste may put you behind for the rest of the day!

45. Journal! It's good for the soul. Write for yourself or create a special journal for your child about his birth and special memories of his childhood. This is guaranteed to put you in a good mood. And what a great gift for your child one day, when he receives a book full of your memories!

46. Make a to-do list for tomorrow. Now, cross off two things that you don't *really* need to do. Entrepreneurial moms are obsessive over-achievers—give yourself a break once in a while!

47. Put a jar or similar container on your kitchen counter. Drop change into it when you arrive home each day. When the kids need lunch money or milk money, send them to the jar.

48. If you have more than one child, purchase towels and plastic plates and cups, allowing each child to have his things in his color. This will alleviate any confusion as to who left the wet towel on the floor or who left the cereal bowl on the kitchen counter. They'll learn quickly to pick up after themselves.

49. If you have a school-age daughter, there is no doubt that you also have dozens of hair bows, barrettes, and clips floating around! To organize the bigger ones, take a thin belt and hang it in her closet with the hair bows and barrettes clipped onto it. To separate and organize the small clips and ponytail holders, use a mini muffin pan that she can keep in a drawer, with all the items in separate compartments.

50. If your family enjoys traveling, purchase a wall map of the United States (or even the world). Let the kids insert a colored pushpin into each new place your family visits.

51. Before your family takes a trip, let your school-age children learn about your destination. They will delight in teaching you about the place you're visiting.

52. Facilitate a book exchange for your children and their friends. It's an inexpensive way to keep them interested in reading, even if you don't have time to go to the library each week.

53. Institute a closed-door policy at your office one day a week. Make it clear to your assistant that unless the building is on fire, you're not to be disturbed. Use this day to catch up. You'll breathe a sigh of relief when you open the door at the end of the day.

54. Paint your office green. It's a soothing color and conducive to problem-solving.

55. Keep a couple of towels in your car. When you're on the run with the kids and stop at a drive-through, have them drape a towel over their lap. When they spill, you'll find this to be not only a time-saver when you can't stop to change their clothes, but also a stress-reducer!

56. Keep a telephone book in your car for quick reference while you're around town or program 1-800-FREE-411 into your cell phone. Paying $2 per cell phone call to directory assistance really adds up in a month's time, and that's money you don't *need* to spend!

57. On Friday evenings, have the whole family spend an hour doing a quick cleanup of the house. Then on Saturday morning, when everyone is running in different directions, there will be less stress for Mom, and everyone benefits from that!

58. Instead of keeping stacks of old magazines because each has an article you want to save, keep only the article from each magazine. Clip each article and mount it on a sheet of paper. Get a three-inch binder and make dividers labeled "Recipes," "Decorating," "Gardening," "Health," "Children," "Finances," etc. Place each article in its coordinating section for easy reference.

59. When you have a houseful of guests and want to cook omelets for breakfast, rather than cooking them one at a time in an omelet pan, try this: Scramble a bowlful of eggs. Chop onions, peppers, cooked ham, etc., and place into individual bowls. Place grated cheese in another bowl. Boil a large pot of water on the stove. Have each person grab a resealable plastic storage bag, and ladle in some eggs and other ingredients of their choice along with a little salt and pepper. Shake well and drop several bags at once into the pot of boiling water. Your omelets will be ready in no time and will come right out of the bag. Plus, the cleanup is quick!

60. Type a permanent sheet of emergency information for your babysitter and keep it beside the telephone or taped inside a cabinet door. Note your cell number, your husband's cell number, the phone numbers of a few trusted neighbors, your pediatrician, and the poison control center. Note whether your children have any known allergies and any medications they're taking. Also list your home's address in case the sitter has to call 911 and your street address does not register on the dispatcher's screen.

61. Hosting your child's birthday party, but running short on time? Ask a friend to help with the decorations and set-up, and then reciprocate when it's her child's birthday. Chances are, she'll enjoy helping you out!

62. No time to write invitations for a children's party? Use your computer and a greeting-card program. Take a few minutes to set up your design, add in the details, then press "Print." If your children are old enough to help, they can stuff the envelopes and even address them. They'll enjoy being able to help, and you can move on to another task at hand.

63. To cut down on the paper clutter in your kitchen, buy a large picture frame for each of your children. Each week, when they bring home their school papers and artwork, let them select a favorite piece to be displayed in their frame.

64. On Sunday afternoon, prepare and wrap or bag snacks and lunch items for the week. Bake your own brownies and cookies from prepared mixes; portion and bag grapes, celery, and cheese cubes. Then, each night as you prepare lunches for the next day, these items are ready.

65. Remove rust from clothing or your pool deck by squeezing lemon juice on the stain, them pouring salt onto the lemon juice.

66. Instead of using ice packs in the kids' lunch, buy a package of bottled water with six to eight bottles per package. Freeze them on Sunday night. They'll keep lunches cool, plus be defrosted and ready to drink by lunchtime.

67. To pack cupcakes in your kids' lunch without smearing the frosting, simply cut the cupcakes in half and spread the frosting in the middle, sandwiched between two sides of the cupcake.

68. Are mornings crazy in your home but you still want to send kids off with a breakfast? On Sunday evening, prepackage cereal, dried fruits, and nuts in resealable plastic bags. They work great for a quick, on-the-go breakfast, when paired with a travel cup of milk as the kids head out the door in the morning!

69. Is the clutter around the house driving you crazy? Enlist the help of your younger school-age children. Assign each child an empty laundry basket and set the kitchen timer for ten minutes. Make a game of it, telling the kids to try to be the first to fill his or her basket with all their own items by the time the timer beeps. (Be sure to have a small treat on hand for the winner, or this won't work next time!)

70. Here's a guaranteed stress-reducer: Take a moment, close your eyes, and remember the sweet smell of your baby's head as you held him close. (Even if your "baby" is now sixteen, I guarantee you can conjure up this precious memory.)

71. Have you ever had a party in your home and awakened the next morning to find oil spots in your driveway from several of your guests' cars? No problem. Grab a can of Coke and pour it onto the spots, then rinse away.

72. Make a point of showing your children how to be charitable. Adopt a less-fortunate family during the holidays. Include your children in the shopping for gifts and holiday meal items. Also let the kids help wrap any presents you will deliver to your adopted family. Then, take the kids along to deliver your goodies, so they can see the results of their kindness.

73. Use liquid body soap in your showers. They leave less residue, allowing for longer times between scrubbing.

74. Keep a squeegee in each shower. Have everyone in your household use it on the glass enclosure and door following their shower. Again, this will allow for longer times between scrubbing!

75. Sleep on a satin pillowcase. You'll get several benefits from this. The first is that your hair will be less tousled in the morning, allowing you to get out the door with less "repair time." And the satin is easier on your skin, causing less "crinkling."

76. Are your kids, and your neighbors' kids, tearing through your kitchen in search of snacks every day after school? Assign a specific cabinet or shelf for kid snacks and keep it stocked. If the kids learn to go to one place, they'll stop rummaging through the pantry and cabinets, leaving a path of destruction in their wake!

77. If you travel frequently, for business or pleasure, keep a travel bag packed with a second set of toiletries, medications, and other essentials. This will save at least fifteen minutes each time you pack.

78. A great stress-reliever during the busy holiday season is to pop a bowl of popcorn and sit down and string it with your kids while watching a classic Christmas movie. Then, go outside and hang the strung popcorn for the birds. Your children will love watching the birds enjoy eating their "gift."

79. If you must use your cell phone while driving and your state allows it, get a hands-free accessory for your phone. This will allow you to keep both hands on the wheel and drive more safely. Plus, it will reduce neck strain. (Common sense says it's best to avoid using your cell phone at all while driving, but all moms know that sometimes it's simply unavoidable. Be safe!)

80. Feeling guilty about overscheduling your kids with sports, scouts, music lessons, and more? You can let go of the guilt. A recent study at Yale University has found that children and teens involved in organized activities for about five hours each week have more functional family relationships, better academic performance, and less substance abuse. So, this is something we're doing right, after all!

81. While it would be impossible to keep every paper and project each of your children brought home from school, you can create a lasting record of it in a tidy scrapbook. After displaying a piece of art for an appropriate amount of time, simply photograph it and have your child insert the photo into his own special album.

82. LifeSavers can really be lifesavers! Keep a roll in your car. When your cell phone rings, quickly pass back the roll to your oldest child, who can dispense the candy. Remind the kids to keep it down while you're on the phone. Mathematically, one LifeSaver is equal to one average telephone call.

83. The LifeSaver trick works great in church, too, to quiet little ones! (Thank you, Grandma, for teaching me this one.)

84. As an entrepreneur, you will need to keep your business-related receipts. Because you're always on the go, it is likely that you will accumulate these receipts in your car. To reduce car clutter, keep several envelopes, labeled "Auto," "Meals," "Job Supplies," etc. Then, once a week, take them into the office.

85. When teaching your teenagers to drive, also teach them to safely change a flat tire and jump start a car's battery with jumper cables. Although nearly everyone has a cell phone today and can call for help, if your teen is on a rural road and can't get a signal, he or she can possibly still remedy their own problem and safely be on their way, even if they can't call for road service.

86. Get your annual flu shot. You don't have time to be sick.

87. Remember to thank your mom for all she does. As a mom yourself, you can now certainly appreciate her years of sacrifice!

88. A great idea for your mom on Mother's Day is to find a pretty decorative, ceramic-type jar with a lid. Then find pretty stationery and

cut it into small pieces. On each piece, write a special thank-you to your mom for something she did for you throughout the course of your lifetime. You'll be amazed at how many memories you have, from her reassurance on your first day of school to her advice on your first date, or even what she did for you last week. And, I can tell you from personal experience, that this gift will be appreciated far more than any gift you could ever buy and wrap. Plus, your mom will get hours of pleasure from reading the special memories you have of her.

89. Keep your business cards accessible at all times. Keep some cards in your purse, your briefcase, your car, your child's diaper bag, your gym bag, and your carry-on luggage. You never know when the opportunity may present itself for you to promote your business to an acquaintance!

90. Always make two sets of backup discs for your computer. Leave one set at the office and take the other set off-site. (You can keep the second set or have your office assistant or bookkeeper take it away from the office.) In the event of a robbery or a natural disaster, you will most likely be able to access at least one set of your discs and have your business records on hand so you can get back to work.

91. After a long day, pumice your feet in the shower. Slather on peppermint lotion. Wear cotton socks to bed and wake with refreshed, soft tootsies in the morning!

92. In a hurry during your morning shower? Distribute conditioner through your hair, and then rub hands on your legs. Now, you're ready for a quick shave, and you won't need to apply lotion.

93. The sound of water has been shown to relax most people. Put a small tabletop fountain in your office.

94. Have a final will and testament prepared so your children are provided for in the event of your untimely death. Arrange with a family member or close friend to take over as guardian and raise your children if you are gone. Spell out your wishes clearly as far as your children are concerned. If finances allow, set up a living trust for your

children. While this may be an unpleasant task, just knowing that it is complete will be a huge stress-reducer.

95. Do you brainstorm while driving? Carry a small handheld tape recorder to record notes for yourself. It's neater than jotting notes on pieces of paper, plus it's much safer while you're driving.

96. Ask your own grandmothers and your mother and mother-in-law to allow you to videotape them as you talk with them individually about their own childhoods, how they met their husbands, the changes they've seen in the world, and any special memories they want to be remembered by the family. Then, make copies of this treasured keepsake and share it with extended family. (My own grandmother died in 1995, but before her death, I made a tape of the two of us talking at her kitchen table, as she shared countless stories of her life. She was born in 1909 and had been witness to so many world-changing events. I felt it was truly a gift to hear about her life in her own words. And, of course, my children now have a priceless gift from their great-grandmother, even though she lived only long enough to meet one of my children.)

97. Keep a digital camera in your vehicle. This way, you'll be sure to have it on hand for your son's football game or your daughter's dance recital. You'll also have it in the event you need it at work to photograph a damaged shipment or to record the pre-existing conditions in a customer's home before your employees begin work. Plus, you'll have it in the event that you are involved in an auto accident and need to document the damage and the conditions. Being prepared is a great stress-reducer.

98. Splurge on a great-fitting, top-quality pair of black slacks. You'll be glad you have them when you need to pull together an outfit in a pinch, and you'll feel great because you'll know you look great.

99. For a priceless "Grandma Gift," help your younger children create an apron or a kitchen tablecloth using their own handprints. Buy an apron at your local craft store or find a plain tablecloth at a department store. Select several small bottles of acrylic paint. Pour paint into separate saucers. Let your child dip his palms into each color, one at a time, and leave his special handprints on his gift for Grandma. (My daughter made an apron for her grandmother when she was about three years old. Today, my daughter is thirteen and still delights in seeing Grandma wear her special apron in the kitchen!)

100. For quick makeup touch-ups while you're getting through your day, carry four basics: mascara, bronzer, lip gloss, and cotton swabs (for quick under-eye smudge cleanups).

101. Take one day a month while the kids are in school and things are under control at the office, and see a movie. You'll feel more relaxed after some alone-time, and your family will enjoy a refreshed mom!

Index

A

accountant, 66, 76, 102, 104

accounts payable, 102

accounts receivable, 97, 99

advertising, 94–96, 112, 118–19

Age Discrimination in Employment
Act of 1967, The, 90

aging report, 102

Ahlers, Joan, 63

allowance, 123

American Business Women's
Association (ABWA), 102

Americans With Disabilities Act of
1990, The, 91

anger, 41

anti-discrimination laws, 90–91

applicants, 91–92

Association of Women's Business
Centers (AWBC), 102

attitude, 36, 37, 48, 70

automobile insurance, 82

B

B&W Motor Company, 70

background checks, 10

balance sheets, 103

Balcom, Kelly, 72

bank accounts, 86

bank fees,m 87

bankers, 86

banking information, 86, 98, 101

Baumler, Tana, 72

Bergerson, Megan, 65

Berrey, Anna, 35

Bocks, Joy, 70

boundaries, 34

Bradshaw, Linda, 59

brochures, 105, 107

business cards, 105–7

business lease, 85

business name, 78, 112

business plan, 88

Business Women's Network (BWN),
102

C

calendars, 70

financing, 88, 102

flexibility, 51, 53, 62–68, 92, 122

forms, employment, 93

franchise, 64, 66

Fresh Baby, 63

friendship, 35

G

general corporation, 79

grand opening, 112–16

gratitude, 96, 118–19

Graves' disease, 33

greeting cards, 96

guilt, 9, 31, 69

H

health, 32–34, 57

hiring, 90–92

holidays, 26

housekeeper, 65, 68

I

Immigration & Naturalization Service (INS), 93

incentives, 94, 106

insurance, 63, 82, 93, 108

International Alliance for Women, The (TIAW), 103

Internet, 78, 91–92, 117–18

interviews 91–92

invoices, 97–98, 100, 102

J

job description, 93

K

KB Creative, 72

Kelly Balcom Designs, 72

key person insurance, 83

L

L & B Services, 70

landlord, 85

late payments, 98

leads, 95, 114

lessee, 85

liability insurance, 82

liens, 98, 101

life insurance, 83

Limited Liability Company (LLC), 80

litigation, 98, 101

location, 84

log, 95–96, 117

logo, 106, 114–15

loss-of-business insurance, 83

Lubbock Adult Day Center, 61

M

Maltby Café, 72

market research, 76–78

marketing plan, 108

marketing, 60, 76, 88, 103, 105, 108, 113, 118

mediocrity, 42

mentoring, 29, 102

merchant services, 87

Molitor, Andrea, 64

motivation, 28, 37, 42, 48, 57, 67, 70

Movin' & Groovin' Exercise for Kids, 66

Acknowledgments

Special thanks to . . .

My family and friends, for their support and patience as I finished this book.

Jerry, without whom I would have never tried entrepreneurship; and Kaitlyn and Jared, for always keeping things in perspective for me. Being your mother has provided me with more love, laughs, and lessons than I could have ever imagined. No matter what else I may do in this lifetime, being your mother is the most rewarding and important of all!

My parents, Kathy and Jack Mathews, for teaching me a good work ethic and the importance of responsibility, both of which I use daily.

Paul Mathews, my "little" brother, whom I can always count on for support, advice, friendship, and love.

Renata Cherapan and Virginia Cunningham, my best friends of twenty-eight years. Your friendship and faith will always be two of the most treasured gifts of my lifetime.

Gloria Davis, for your love and support over the years, and especially for your son, whom I am blessed to have as my husband.

Some other moms I've admired for their approach to motherhood; their selflessness; and their strength: Mimi, Kathy, Gloria, Judy, Bobbie, Renata, Virginia, Mary Lynn, Joan, Cheriee, Tina, Marsha, Stacy, Judie, Linda, Jodi, Julli, Andrea, and Sharon. Your children are so fortunate to have each of you!

All of the incredible entrepreneurial moms featured in this book. Your honest and heartfelt input will be invaluable to other moms who want a glimpse of entrepreneurship, as they consider taking the giant leap themselves. Thank you so much, ladies, for your time and your inspiration!

And a huge thanks to Ron Pitkin and Cumberland House Publishing, for not only giving a voice to one entrepreneurial mom, but for opening the door to countless others!

About the Author

Mary Davis has owned and managed her own flooring business since 1992. She lives with her husband and two children in Cocoa, Florida.